Show Me the Proof

Tools and Strategies to Make Data Work for You

Show Me the Proof

Tools and Strategies to Make Data Work for You

With a Foreword by Douglas B. Reeves

Stephen H. White

A L P
**Advanced
Learning
Press**

Advanced Learning Press

317 Inverness Way South, Suite 150

Englewood, CO 80112

Phone (800) 844-6599 or (303) 504-9312 ▪ Fax (303) 504-9417

www.MakingStandardsWork.com/Advanced_Learning_Press.html

Library of Congress Cataloging-in-Publication Data:

White, Stephen H.; 1949 –

    Show me the proof! : tools and strategies to make data work for you / Stephen H. White

      p. cm.

Companion handbook for: Beyond the numbers.

Includes bibliographical references and index.

    ISBN 0-9709455-9-0 (pbk.)

    1. Educational statistics—United States.   2. Educational indicators—United States.   3. Educational evaluation—United States.   4. Educational accountability—United States.   I. Title: Beyond the numbers.   II. Title.

LB2846.W4394   2005

379.1'58—dc22   2004062678

Printed in the United States of America

10 09 08 07 06 05   01 02 03 04 05 06 07 08 09

Dedicated to my wife, Linda,

whose patience, encouragement,

and love add value to all I do.

Contents

Foreword   ix

Acknowledgments   xiii

About the Author   xv

Introduction   xvii

1   Evidence to Satisfy the Skeptic   1

2   Types of Data   21

3   A Data Road Map   33

4   Methods for Data Analysis   49

5   Triangulation   67

6   Replication   77

7   Data and Leadership   85

APPENDICES

A   Critical Incident Analysis   95

B   Collaboration Checklist   97

C   Relations Diagram   99

D   Assessment Calendar   101

E   Acts of Accountability   103

F   SWOT/Data Team Analysis   105

G   Scoring Guide Matrix for Analysis of Data   107

H   A Data Road Map   121

I   Data Analysis and Principles   133

J   Flowcharting   135
        Flowchart Components   136
        Deployment Flowchart and Assessment Calendar Interface   137
        Flowchart and Process Map Path to Excellence   138

K   Venn Diagram   139

L   Force-Field Analysis   141

M   Decision Matrix   143

N   Clarification Analysis   145

O   Triangulation   147
        Template for Triangulation of Data   147

P   Wagon Wheel   149
        Steps in Using Wagon Wheels   150
        Wagon-Wheel Tool for Data Analysis   151

Q   The Hishakawa Fishbone: A Cause-and-Effect Diagram   153

R   Group Norms for Meetings and Data Analysis   155

S   Control, Run, and Discrepancy Charts   157

T   Side-by-Side Analysis   159

U   Listening System   161
        Part I: Stakeholder Satisfaction   162
        Part II: Focus Groups and Structured Interviews   163
        Part III: Web Site   164

V   Plus/Delta (+/Δ) Group Processing Tool   165

W   Logarithmic Chart for Forecasting   167

Glossary   169

References   173

Index   177

Foreword

Douglas B. Reeves, Ph.D.

his was the best professional development experience of my life—our faculty and administrators are more inspired and excited than I have seen them in years." These are the words of a senior educational leader after hearing Dr. Stephen White present the information you now hold in your hands. In this important book, Dr. White focuses the attention of educators and school leaders on precisely the right place: the facts. In an era when discussions of education are frequently dominated by political rhetoric, this book reminds us that the children we serve are best served when we put aside our predispositions, politics, and prejudices and let our professional practice be guided by some fundamental questions, such as:

- How well are schools in our community performing?
- How well is *my* school performing?
- What can my colleagues and I do to capitalize on our strengths?
- How can we recognize our challenges in a constructive and nondefensive way?
- Are state test scores the only source of data on student achievement?
- What does "proof" in the context of education mean anyway?

With compelling evidence from an impressive variety of sources, the author helps us to address these and a host of other questions. Best of all, *Show Me the Proof!* helps us to discover our own answers. Although the research of other scholars is important, the fundamental argument of this book is that effective teachers and school leaders must accumulate evidence from a variety of sources, including their own observations and practices, in order to satisfy skeptics and themselves that the decisions they are making to improve student achievement are sound. Though perfection in decision-making will always elude us, the author makes clear that our profession can and must do a much better job of translating data into action.

There are some books—the poems of Dylan Thomas, a David McCullough biography, or a Dostoevsky novel—that can be read in solitary delight. But data analysis is a team sport, and a careful study of this book will require a collaborative effort. The tools and checklists in every chapter can be powerful tools for discovery and the improvement of achievement, but that potential will remain dormant if those tools lie unused. Therefore, while you may be enjoying a solitary reading of this book now, your efforts will be far more effective if you make this volume a whole-faculty book study, taking time to linger over each chapter, complete each exhibit, and follow the collaborative principles in its pages. As teachers and educational leaders, we are in a learning profession and serve learning organizations.

The duty we have to our students, our employers, our colleagues, and ourselves is above all a duty to learn. Few roles in life are as transparent as the enterprise of teaching, in which every mood and subliminal attitude is telegraphed to our students. They know when we are modeling intellectual curiosity and when we share the intense desire to learn and grow that we hope they will emulate. They also know when we are exhausted and disengaged. One of the things I like best about this book is that it can restore some of the sheer joy of discovery and learning in a context where that joy rarely happens: faculty meetings and professional development seminars in schools.

Much has been written about data analysis in the past few years. The topic is perhaps second only to "leadership" as one for which entire forests have been sacrificed in the service of unhelpful publications. The two things that make this book stand out from the rest are its practicality and its rigor. We are spared endless platitudes and given clear and direct action plans. Because he respects his readers—after all, Dr. White is a veteran teacher and school leader, as well as a prolific author and respected researcher—he does not talk down to us. The analytical rigor he brings to student achievement is far more challenging than "looking at the test scores" or "focusing on your weaknesses." Every overwhelmed teacher and leader will particularly appreciate the very direct link between data analysis and specific solutions. Dr. White challenges educational policy makers and senior administrators to give explicit permission to teachers and principals to make key changes in curriculum, teaching practices, classroom assessment, and resource allocation. The author speaks for legions of his profession when he reminds those in authority that they cannot hold teachers and principals accountable without providing explicit decisionmaking authority to correspond to that accountability.

This is one of those rare books in which every page, including the exhibits and appendices, is important. Several of the appendices are particularly helpful, as they provide simple tools (including a rich variety of forms) that will help focus professional development seminars, meetings, and any forum of teachers and leaders on the most important elements of teaching, achievement, curriculum, and leadership. At the start of every chapter, the author has provided a quotation of historical interest and current relevance. I will follow his example with the words of the founder of Taoism, the Chinese philosopher Lao Tzu. Writing twenty-seven centuries ago in the

Tao Te Ching, he captured the essence of the effective use of this book, reminding us that neither leaders nor authors can substitute for the collaborative wisdom that you and your colleagues will bring to the enterprise before us. He wrote:

> Of the best leaders, . . . when their task is accomplished, their work done, the people all remark, "'We have done it ourselves.'"

My wish for you is that in future years, as you reflect on the challenges you faced and overcame and the successes that you, your colleagues, and your students have accomplished, each of you will say with confidence, "We did it ourselves."

Swampscott, Massachusetts

Dr. Reeves is the author of nineteen books and was twice named to the Harvard University Distinguished Authors Series. He is the founder of the Center for Performance Assessment.

Acknowledgments

how Me the Proof! is the companion handbook to *Beyond the Numbers,* a fresh look at data analysis that makes a compelling argument for the teacher's expert role in data analysis. *Beyond the Numbers* was written to provide a framework within which teachers and school leaders can make data work for them, rather than having them be at the beck and call of data. It provides templates for listening systems, assessment calendars, and recipes for replication; more importantly, it expands the understanding of data beyond student achievement results on state and national assessments to include the antecedents of excellence and collective wisdom of educators in the field. *Show Me the Proof!* is intended to translate that collective wisdom into hard evidence through practical analysis tools, methods of analysis, and guidelines for excellence.

Neither book would have been written without the help and encouragement of educational leaders across the nation who continue to pursue a deeper level of data analysis.

I'm indebted, as are so many, to Dr. Douglas Reeves for his vision and encouragement; to Anne Fenske for her ability to see possibilities most of us miss; and to my many colleagues at the Center for Performance Assessment, who respond with agility to meet the changing needs of schools and other organizations every day. In my thirty-third year as an educator, my association with this extraordinary organization continues to demonstrate how respect, fairness, teamwork, reason, and excellence can exist simultaneously, and how good ideas can have great impact when one doesn't care who receives the credit.

No acknowledgment would be complete without a reference to my wife Linda, whose common sense and ability to see the forest for the trees helped me clarify key elements as the book was created; and to our eight children, whose ambitions and unfolding lives make every day one worth celebrating

About the Author

Stephen H. White, Ed.D.

tephen White, Ed.D., is no stranger to data analysis. His career spans more than thirty years in three countries and four states, serving preschool to graduate students in public and private education since 1972. Raised in Montana, he received his Doctorate in Educational Leadership from Montana State University in 1989.

Dr. White's career has been characterized by creation of innovative programs in response to emerging needs, high-quality fiscal stewardship of limited public resources, and a consistent focus on professional development and best practice. As a teacher, counselor, coordinator, director, high school principal, chief executive officer of a higher education BOCES, executive director, assistant superintendent, and superintendent, Dr. White has had the privilege of being involved in significant reform initiatives and hands-on experience with the day-to-day challenges of leadership in public education, all of which required insightful data management and analysis.

Previous publications include ten journal articles and a contribution to a university textbook, addressing subjects as diverse as the transition from school to work, performance excellence, and finding common ground in a diverse and divided society. Dr. White is the author of the Center for Performance Assessment's seminar on "Advanced Data-Driven Decision Making," and he is proud to be associated with the world's preeminent source of professional development in the areas of standards, assessment, and accountability.

Show Me the Proof! and its companion book, *Beyond the Numbers,* represent his practical experience, depth of knowledge, and innovation in this timely and challenging topic.

He resides in Highlands Ranch, Colorado, with his wife, Linda, and youngest son, Jonathan, enjoying skiing, cycling, grandchildren, and a good spy novel whenever time allows.

Dr. White can be reached at swhite@MakingStandardsWork.com.

Introduction

Show Me the Proof! is the companion handbook to *Beyond the Numbers;* both books are designed for the educator who desires the tools and strategies to make visible the invisible in today's charged, high-stakes environment. A quick check of all fifty state department of education Web sites reveals that every school district, every elementary and secondary school, and every charter school is now issued a report card that is disseminated widely to the public. Some school districts, concerned about the manner in which data is provided to citizens, spend time and money to issue a parallel report card during the same time frame, presumably to correct any errors or misconceptions that might result from the state report cards.

Show Me the Proof! is written for practitioners who labor under a growing demand for data and improved results but find few models for analyzing the data already available to them. *Show Me the Proof!* is designed to offer practical, user-friendly tools and strategies that allow educators to respond to the data, and to manage it from collection to implementation to evaluation of their data systems—and to do so with confidence in their unique understanding of teaching and learning.

Each chapter includes specific applications of the tools of analysis (found in the appendices at the end of the book). *Show Me the Proof!* is both a handbook of tools and a resource for ideas; as such, it is my profound hope that practitioners in the field find that *Show Me the Proof!* allows them to develop a preponderance of evidence linking results with the antecedents that cause them, and to accomplish what they alone are capable of doing. Only teachers and principals can translate data into action, modify practices based on sound data, engage students to apply their best thinking, and ultimately improve student achievement.

Evidence to Satisfy
the Skeptic

To be persuasive, we must be believable; to be believable we must be credible; to be credible, we must be truthful.

—EDWARD R. MURROW (1908–1965)

The public wants proof that its schools are performing. In fact, "show me the proof" could be the subtitle for the No Child Left Behind Act of 2001 (Pub. L. No. 107-110) (NCLB Act), because the federal government, through the states, is sending a message: "No longer will your accreditation processes or even your self-selected standardized tests suffice to convince us that schools are doing well. From now on, you had better 'show me the proof!'" In these early years of the twenty-first century, your school must demonstrate that students in all subgroups are learning, and that learning gaps between each subgroup and the overall population will be eliminated by a specific time. Otherwise, you risk losing the autonomy and authority to manage, and perhaps teach, at the school you love. Few would be surprised to find that faculty and staff members are not too thrilled with this new scrutiny (Sunderman, Tracey, Kim, & Orfield, 2004, 28). Despite numerous and vociferous protestations, the only definitive indicator of effectiveness applied to determine incentives or sanctions is the sum of test scores students achieve on external—and rigorous—assessments. To the general public, *tests matter.*

This book is designed to turn the tables somewhat; to provide educators with the tools and strategies that will evidence their effectiveness, quite apart from annual state assessments. *Show Me the Proof!* is designed to empower educators with a preponderance of evidence that historically has not been reduced to writing or leveraged as data. This transformation is neither magic nor imaginary. It is the result of applying the right tools of analysis to the right types of data for the right purposes. The goal is nothing less than having professionals reach the point where external state assessments are used primarily to corroborate what educators already know is working. Rather than relying on a state assessment to validate and legitimize their work, educators legitimize their craft by developing measures of teaching, learning, and improving that represent antecedents of excellence, best practices, proven conditions for learning, and teacher behaviors that are embedded and used every day in classrooms and schools.

You may be thinking, "That's a nice idea, but if you think the general public or parents I work with are going to accept my version of proof, you surely must have fallen off a turnip truck in the not-too-distant past. I wasn't born yesterday." I agree: not about the turnip truck, but about your general assessment. Proof must have the stature of objectivity, serve as evidence, and present a convincing argument to the skeptic.

Proof is a very elusive thing, as illustrated by the "knowing–doing" gap, a trend prevalent in too many schools today (Reeves, 2004a; Sparks, 2004; Auman & Young, 2004). There is ample evidence of what works in schools, yet the most effective strategies, programs, and structures are implemented unevenly and far too rarely. Linda Auman and Karen Young systematically observed 1,500 classrooms in 2004 and found that only 4 percent had clear learning objectives and only 3 percent used activities that required higher-order thinking; 52 percent relied on worksheets during the classroom observation. This despite the fact that the literature is replete with proven practices! Exhibit 1.1 cites twenty educational practices that have been demonstrated to be effective, both in the literature (Marzano, Pickering, & Pollock, 2001a; Reeves, 2004b; Tomlinson, 2001; Danielson, 1996; Heacox, 2002; Gregory & Chapman, 2002) and in the field. I captured these antecedents and those applied by practitioners as a result of a wide range of Center for Performance Assessment seminars in *Beyond the Numbers* (White, 2005, 148).

Lucy Steiner (2000) identifies several reasons why educators are especially reluctant to "upscale" or replicate practices that have been "proven," by a preponderance of the evidence, to make a difference. One particularly troubling reason was the need for large groups of educators to "unlearn" the assumptions that underlie their current work— work designed for a different era, a time when data was a necessary inconvenience rather than a central component of reform and school improvement.

The knowing–doing gap is a problem everyone in education can recognize. Graham, Harris, Fink-Chorzempa & MacArthur (2003, 279) describe how only 42 percent of teachers, when presented compelling evidence about the power of nonfiction writing with editing and revision to improve achievement in all areas, made any adaptations at all for poor writers. Only 10 percent utilized the strategies of mini-lessons, tutoring, and revised instruction that were presented to primary teachers as the very antecedents that led to improved achievement. As a profession, we struggle with applying the lessons from the research that shout at us about leveraging numerous antecedents of excellence. Douglas Reeves attributes this reluctance not to indifference or even unwillingness, but to frustration from looking in the wrong places (2004b, 2). James Surowiecki, in *The Wisdom of Crowds*, found people reluctant to accept evidence until they tested

Exhibit 1.1	Compelling Antecedents of Excellence: Proof of Practitioners
Structures, Conditions, and Teacher Behaviors Worth Replicating	**Categories of Effective Teaching Strategies**
■ More writing, thinking, analysis, and reading, in every content area	■ Identifying similarities and differences
■ Collaborative scoring of student work	■ Summarizing and note taking
■ Flexible schedules and greater investment of time in basic sources; associated with lower failure rates	■ Reinforcing effort and providing recognition
■ More frequent feedback; associated with improved student work ethic, motivation, and performance	■ Using homework and practice
	■ Using nonlinguistic representations
■ Collaboration structures for analysis of data	■ Using cooperative learning
	■ Setting objectives and providing feedback
■ Creation and use of data teams; increase in the presence of effective teaching strategies; increase in student achievement	■ Generating and testing hypotheses
	■ Using questions, cues, and advance organizers to increase student cognition and engagement
■ Discussion of, review of, and focus on actual student work; close the learning gap for all cohort groups	■ Differentiating instruction
■ Learning logs to collaboratively monitor student progress	
■ Mandatory department teams with responsibility and authority for selecting effective strategies and developing and evaluating end-of-course (EOC) assessments	
■ Relentless focus on student achievement	
■ Protection of time	
■ Deep professional development	

the new process themselves (2004, 61–62). Most of us are by nature skeptics; that is, people who have learned through experience that acceptance of something on its face without sufficient scrutiny is a sure-fire way to be "had" by the latest fad or, perhaps, by the latest cad. Proof is personal. So, what *does* constitute proof?

In the legal profession, the common standard of proof in civil cases is a preponderance of the evidence. The *burden of proof,* defined as the obligation to prove an assertion, consists of three elements: circumstantial evidence, satisfaction of the burden of production or evidence, and the burden of persuasion (Britannica Concise Encyclopedia,

2004). Thus, the process requires sufficient evidence to suggest that something may be true (circumstantial evidence); physical evidence of the alleged events, actions, or omissions; and a compelling-enough case to persuade a neutral and otherwise skeptical audience (e.g., a jury, school board, or advisory committee). As citizens of a well-established democracy, these standards prevail in almost all disputes, whether as to ideas or as to property and person. Educators, however, as one might expect, have their own definitions of *proof.*

Publishers, anxious to satisfy existing research requirements for reading under the NCLB Act, have begun to invest considerable sums to turn out products that: (1) validate the pedagogy behind their products, or explain why it should work; and (2) provide research that demonstrates the effectiveness of their products (Mickey, 2003). Mike Schmoker notes, "Educators are hungry for both kinds of detail: evidence of exactly how a method works as well as concrete descriptions of how to make it work" (1999, 53). Douglas Reeves refers to a body of evidence in mutiple contexts, from standards to decision making (2000b, 5–19). Edie Holcomb, in *Getting Excited about Data,* calls for proof based on evidence of implementation and impact (2004, 201). It is clear that whether the subject arena is the classroom, the operating room, the courtroom, or the board room, proof is a multifaceted construct that includes physical evidence, persuasive argument, and a logical connection to purpose and application. Thus, throughout this book, we use a definition of *proof* as meeting the following three standards:

1. A compelling rationale: Circumstantial evidence; a preponderance of evidence that implies the conclusion

2. Means to satisfy the skeptics: Physical evidence of improvement and context

3. A persuasive argument: External evidence that corroborates the rationale and affirms the physical evidence

Teachers need to offer proof of their successes beyond test scores. *Show Me the Proof!* is about developing skills in data analysis that allow each professional to understand the data of teaching, learning, improving, and persuading, and to structure the instructional program to improve his or her ability in each data arena. The following sections review three principles of data-driven decision making, describe the negative consequences of the rearview-mirror effect, and offer the educator's version of "canaries in the coal mine."

BEDROCK PRINCIPLES OF DATA ANALYSIS

Three principles are absolutely critical to successful data analysis and the capacity to make decisions on the basis of that analysis: collaboration, antecedents, and accountability.

Collaboration

Collaboration powerful enough to drive excellence in student achievement has three characteristics: (1) it is present from planning to execution in data-driven decision making; (2) it helps develop team thinking and candor in data-driven decision making; and (3) it is integrated into every data-driven decision. Collaboration provides a forum to legitimize proposed changes, and promotes insights that numbers alone are unable to produce. Exhibit 1.2 describes analysis tools for collaboration.

Critical incident analysis is a means of gaining the collective wisdom of stakeholders when identifying key issues for further analysis and action. Exhibit 1.3 depicts how

Exhibit 1.2

Analysis Tools Aligned to Characteristics of Collaboration

Tool for Analysis	Characteristic of Collaboration
Critical incident	Team thinking and candor
Collaboration checklist for integrated decision making	Integrated data-driven decision making
Relations diagram	Team thinking and candor
Assessment calendar	Explicit steps from planning to execution

Exhibit 1.3

Critical Incident as a Collaborative Tool

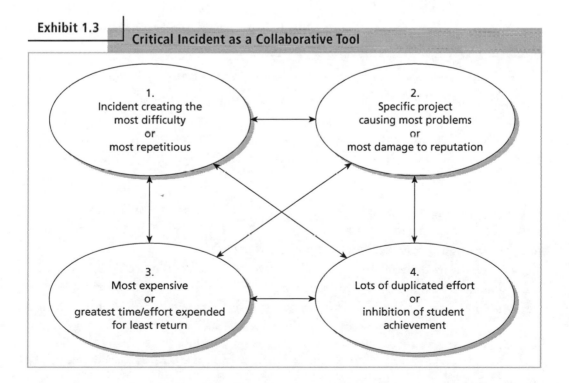

collaboration can produce high-quality insights just by examining critical incidents. A tool for root-cause analysis (Andersen & Fagerhaug, 2000, 23), this method brings issues to the forefront and jump-starts analysis based on the insights that emerge from collaboration. Not one shred of student achievement data is introduced initially, but the process puts the spotlight on the kinds of data that will have to be addressed for sustained school success.

The process for determining a "critical incident" is simple and effective. Large groups, or teams as small as two persons, examine each dichotomy separately, then prioritize from the four choices what is most urgent, most compelling, and most important to address first. Critical incident analysis jump-starts data analysis by using the collective wisdom of the group to identify priorities. (A template with instructions is provided in Appendix A.)

The *checklist for integrated decision making* (see Exhibit 1.4) ensures a collaborative effort, because it asks participants to consider the degree to which the collaborative structure has been implemented. As you review the checklist, confer with a colleague to add other items or modify the checklist items to strengthen collaboration in your setting. (A template for the collaboration checklist is found in Appendix B.)

The third tool of analysis is similar to critical incident, but is used for the purpose of discovering relationships rather than bringing issues to the forefront or establishing priorities. The main purpose of a *relations diagram* is to help identify relationships that are not easily recognizable. There are five steps in the process:

1. Determine the factors to be analyzed (events, quantitative data, functions).

2. Place the factors in empty chart boxes.

3. Assign arrows to illustrate whether those factors impact other factors or are impacted by them in the relationship.

4. Count the arrows proceeding to and from each factor.

5. Identify factors that impact more areas than the number of times they are impacted by other factors; these are *drivers*. Those that are impacted more frequently are *indicators*.

Relations diagrams are useful in determining relationships among curriculum, specific standards, and subgroup performance patterns. Exhibit 1.5 provides an example of a relations diagram in a typical high school classroom.

The relations diagram in Exhibit 1.5 identifies NCLB sanctions and rewards, state assessment results, and school report cards as the primary drivers in the relationship among the six variables. The NCLB system affects five other areas but is not itself affected by any of the other variables; the school report card affects four areas but is affected only by the NCLB system. In this example, the external state and federal mandates drive class size, textbook selection, curriculum alignment, and professional development.

Exhibit 1.4	Collaboration Checklist for Data Analysis				
Integrating Collaboration into Data Systems	**P**	**I**	**E**	**Additional Ways to Integrate Collaboration?**	
Recommendations are reviewed only when submitted with peers.				_____	
Collaborative schedules provide common planning and teaming.				_____	
Teacher teams examine student work prior to designing interventions.				_____	
Common assessments are designed, developed, and evaluated by collaborative teams.				_____	
Leader requests analysis with recommendations for specific students.				_____	
Assessment calendars establish times for collaboration in analysis, reflection, action planning, and implementation.				_____	
Early release times are devoted to collaboration around student work.				_____	
Time and effort are reallocated to respond to urgent challenges identified as a result of collaboration.				_____	
A collaborative process is used to select instructional strategies for each urgent challenge.				_____	
A data analysis road map is in place.				_____	
Faculty, department, and grade-level teams systematically engage in collaborative processes to find solutions.				_____	
Professional development is driven by data re student performance and teaching quality.				_____	

P – Proposed   I = Introduced   E = Established

What are the implications of the relations diagram? At the very least, it warrants a revisiting of goals and objectives to make sure sufficient attention is given to those external and public results. It should assist in increased scrutiny as to textbook selection, professional development selection, and curriculum alignment. Once again, the collaborative nature of the tool drives the analysis, as professionals contribute their best thinking in a structured way. Were test scores necessary to apply this tool? Like

Exhibit 1.5

Relations Diagram

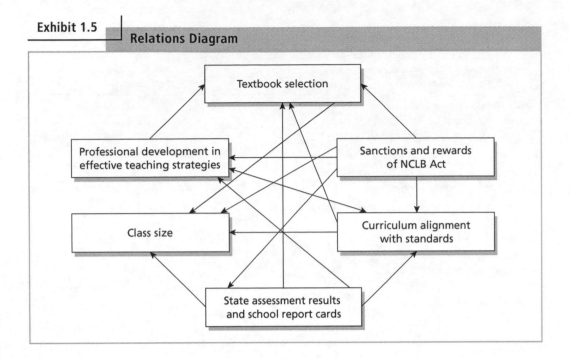

critical incident, a relations diagram helps us understand how our current system works through professional judgment, inviting further analysis and verification with data, but introducing new understanding in the process. Appendix C contains a template for the relations diagram.

The fourth tool of collaboration is perhaps the most critical, because it ensures that sufficient analysis takes place for every important assessment. The checklist, relations diagram, and critical incident tools all offer insights that require further verification before action is taken. The assessment calendar ensures that every step in a comprehensive data analysis process takes place in a timely manner that responds to the lessons of the data on behalf of students. Exhibit 1.6 shows an assessment calendar (templates are provided in Appendix D). The assessment calendar sets aside time for the nine collaborative action steps included in the analysis of assessment data. Note how the assessments are spaced throughout the year to provide time for collection, analysis, reflection, decisions, and transparent communication to stakeholders.

Assessment calendars should be tailored to the realities of external mandates and still provide time for quality data collection analysis, reflection, recommendations, decisions, and action. However, recommended times for completion of analysis steps are supplied. The example also includes a recommended assessment to subtract from the district battery (see strike-throughs). The criterion-referenced test (CRT) is recommended for elimination because: (1) it competes for testing windows with other assessments that are more aligned with standards, such as EOC and writing assessments; and (2) CRTs can be folded into EOC, textbook, and unit common assessments. The

Exhibit 1.6   Assessment Calendar

Assessment	Administration	Collection Date/Window	Disaggregation Date/Window	Analysis	Reflection	Recommendation of Changes	Decision Point	Written Rationale	Dissemination to Stakeholders
NRT	Sept. 10–14	Sept. 17–21	Sept. 17–21	Sept. 24	Sept. 25	Sept. 27	Sept. 28	Oct. 3	Oct. 5
State assessment	Mar. 4–18	Mar. 21–28	Mar. 29–Apr. 8	Apr. 11	Apr. 12	Apr. 13	Apr. 14	Apr. 18	Apr. 20
~~CRTs~~	~~Oct. 1–8~~ ~~May 2–4~~	~~Pretest~~ ~~May 5~~	~~Pretest~~ ~~May 6~~	~~Pretest~~ ~~May 9~~	~~Pretest~~ ~~May 10~~	~~Pretest~~ ~~May 11~~	~~Pretest~~ ~~May 12~~	~~Pretest~~ ~~May 13~~	~~Pretest~~ ~~June 10~~
Writing assessment	Oct. 15–19 Apr. 25–29	Pretest May 2	Pretest May 3	Pretest May 4	Pretest May 5	Pretest May 6	Pretest May 9	Pretest May 10	Pretest June 10
EOC assessments	Jan. 21–23 May 9–11	Jan. 24 May 12	Jan. 24 May 12	Jan. 25 May 13	Jan. 25 May 16	Jan. 28 May 17	Jan. 29 May 18	Jan. 30 May 18	Feb. 5 June 10
Common assessments	Last Fri. of Sept./Nov./Feb.	First Mon. of Oct./Dec./Mar.	First Mon. of Oct./Dec./Mar.	First Tues. of Oct./Dec./Mar.	First Wed. of Oct./Dec./Mar.	First Thurs. of Oct./Dec./Mar.	First Fri. of Oct./Dec./Mar.	First Fri. of Oct./Dec./Mar.	Optional
Performance assessments	Ongoing, at least 1/term/core subject	Ongoing, seamless	Ongoing, seamless	Ongoing, seamless	Ongoing, seamless	Ongoing, seamless	Ongoing, seamless	Ongoing, seamless	Ongoing, seamless
Unit tests	No more than 2 Weds./month	Same day	Same day	Same day	Same day	Second day	Second day	Second day	Optional
Other	Teacher-determined	N/A	N/A	N/A	N/A	N/A	N/A	N/A	N/A

- Scheduled times to collect, aggregate, and disaggregate data
- Required time for analysis, reflection, and recommendations for changes
- Decision points to proceed with status quo or implement change recommendations
- Written rationale for each decision
- Disseminate rationale driven by data to all affected parties

assessment calendar allows teams at all levels to make decisions on the basis of which assessments will provide the most meaningful information to them. Because the teams examine all assessments, the calendar helps eliminate overlap and the tendency to overtest in the attempt to be thorough.

Antecedents

The next principle of data analysis is the management and leverage of antecedents to produce excellence in performance, processes, and student achievement. *Antecedents* are those structures and conditions that precede, anticipate, or predict excellence in performance. They lead to excellence in student achievement, excellence in implementing a new program or strategy, or excellence in performing routine tasks. Antecedents are teaching strategies such as questioning, reinforcing effort, rewarding achievement, and instruction in nonlinguistic representation.

Antecedents are also causes that correlate with effects in student behavior and achievement (results), such as classroom routines or grading procedures. The degree of consistency with which standards are implemented in the classroom has a direct effect on student behaviors. Hence, we refer to these routine practices and teacher behaviors as *causes*.

Antecedents also include conditions such as class size, technology literacy, availability of textbooks, and existence of structures such as continued education unit (CEU) requirements, block scheduling, data teams, and prescribed data reflection times.

Exhibit 1.7

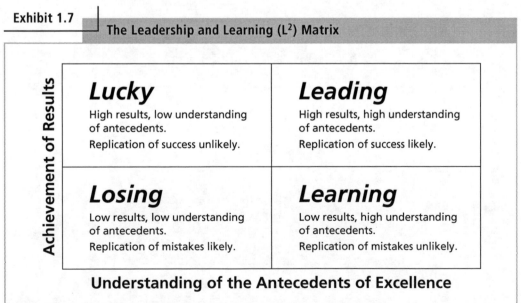

The Leadership and Learning (L²) Matrix

Lucky High results, low understanding of antecedents. Replication of success unlikely.	**Leading** High results, high understanding of antecedents. Replication of success likely.
Losing Low results, low understanding of antecedents. Replication of mistakes likely.	**Learning** Low results, high understanding of antecedents. Replication of mistakes unlikely.

Achievement of Results (vertical axis)

Understanding of the Antecedents of Excellence (horizontal axis)

Source: Reprinted with permission from Douglas B. Reeves, Ph.D.

All influence achievement. Dr. Douglas Reeves created a simple but elegant matrix describing the relationship between antecedents and student achievement. Exhibit 1.7 outlines his Leadership-Learning (L^2) Matrix, and is reprinted with Dr. Reeves's generous permission.

The reader will quickly note that the leader's effectiveness (teacher, principal, parent) is really a function of his or her understanding of the antecedents that actually lead to improved student achievement. If results are low, but the leader (e.g., teacher) understands what is needed to improve student achievement, he will learn from the mistakes that produced the poor performance, and he will be unlikely to repeat the mistakes. On the opposite quadrant is the leader (e.g., principal) who is euphoric about the excellent performance of students at her school but has very little understanding of what produced those scores this year. As a result, replication of that success is very unlikely and the euphoria will quickly fade. The matrix is a powerful reminder that what we as educators do matters, and that we need to gather sufficient data on those things we can change or influence to produce improved student achievement: the data of teaching, learning, improving, and persuading.

Accountability

The final principle of data analysis is *accountability:* taking responsibility to act on the basis of what data tells us. A medical analogy helps illustrate that concept. When a child has a temperature of 103 degrees, few of us would wait until the next morning to take action, let alone the next week. To even consider waiting until next semester would be unconscionable—yet schools routinely make such decisions. In schools, the data shouts, "Intervene, take action!," but a common response is to dismiss it with, "We tried that before." Accountability regarding data analysis means, first and foremost, taking action on the basis of what the data tells us and acting quickly on the diagnosis rather than allowing the problem to persist and fester. Accountability is student-centered (Reeves, 2004b, 6): it relies on measures of both student achievement and antecedents of excellence. Accountability means that teachers provide leadership in the analysis process and that such leadership is fundamentally collaborative in its application. We will define it this way:

> *Accountability* is authority to commit resources (to take action), responsibility to demonstrate improvement (results), and permission to adjust time and opportunity (permission to subtract) so that all students achieve beyond their expectations and the expectations of adults committed to their achievement (parents, teachers, other educators).

A thumbnail definition of *accountability* for data analysis is simply:

> Authority to act, permission to subtract, and responsibility for results.

The authority to take action is central to accountability and an ethical considera-tion as well. Collecting, disaggregating, analyzing, and reflecting are important elements in the process of data analysis, but failure to take action and make necessary changes is patently unethical. That failure requires students and staff to behave as if something will be done with the test data, when in fact the data may be collected and shelved, or analyzed for the sake of analysis. Such communication may not be dishonest or illegal, but it is definitely unethical. A key question regarding the South Asia tsunami tragedy at the end of 2004 concerned the presence or availability of advance warning: Did those with the knowledge of the earthquake take action on the basis of that data? Given the scope of that tragedy, one can see that the authority to act cannot be separated from accountability.

A recent and quite serious proposal was made to revamp how educators measure teacher effectiveness. By issuing each teacher a unique identification number and gath-ering the right data, states can assess the link between teacher performance and student outcomes over the course of many years (Raymond, 2003). Acceptance of inequality as chance or luck in terms of teacher assignment may even be actionable in a court of law. Exhibit 1.8 describes opportunities where leaders of teachers and teachers of students need the authority to act—and act *now.*

Exhibit 1.8 implies that teachers and principals must be given authority to change the time allotted for students to reach proficiency, adding time for those who need more

Exhibit 1.8

Ten Actions of Accountability

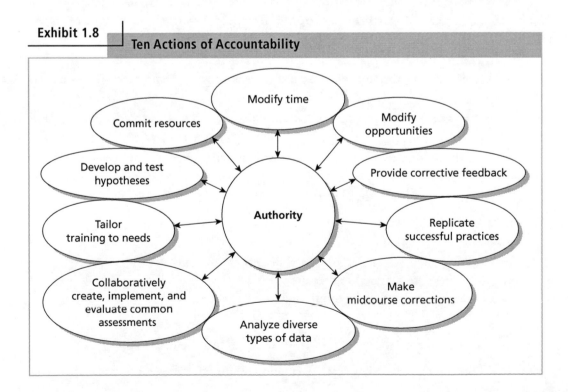

instruction or practice, and redirecting time for those who quickly demonstrate proficiency on a particular standard. Why isn't such authority to become accountable the norm? The answer, in part, is that educators do not maintain sufficiently informative data to warrant granting that authority, or even to justify their own recommendations. Data is as necessary for accountability to operate as accountability is necessary for a quality data system. Exhibit 1.9 identifies common barriers to accountability and provides possible remedies that ensure educators have the authority needed for true accountability. A template to identify the acts of authority in your setting is provided in Appendix E.

These ten acts of accountability provide explicit structures to empower educators to make needed changes. Without permission to subtract obsolete practices, many educators will continue to adhere to past expectations. We assume that others know when they have permission to make changes. Do teachers you are familiar with have authority (permission) to make these decisions?

- Permission to vary the time given to curriculum content
- Permission to modify or accelerate curriculum based on individual student needs, including permission for students to test out of various units or sections
- Permission to replace grades with scoring guides describing proficiency
- Permission to provide multiple opportunities to demonstrate proficiency, as opposed to one try on key tests and assessments
- Permission to integrate assessments across curriculum areas
- Permission to team-teach rather than deliver instruction independent of one's peers

It is as true for administrators as it is for teachers. Do administrators in schools you are familiar with have authority (permission) to make the following decisions?

- Permission to reassign staff midyear
- Permission to hire staff from those who meet all district criteria
- Permission to change teacher assignments based on student achievement data
- Permission to require side-by-side analyses of standards, assessments, curriculum, and lesson plans
- Permission to direct resources to create additional time and opportunity
- Permission to replace textbooks with laptops, or to use textbooks as supplemental material, relying primarily on standards-based performance assessments

These examples illustrate that many times educators have very limited authority or permission to subtract ineffective practices. Accountability is responsibility for results, but without the authority to commit resources and permission to subtract obsolete or

Exhibit 1.9

Barriers to the Ten Acts of Accountability

Act of Accountability	Barriers	Remedies
Commit resources	▪ One-size-fits-all work schedules for assistants ▪ Limited school or department budgets ▪ Negotiated agreement limits ▪ Transportation issues	▪ Allocate assistant time based on data trends for service needs ▪ Insist that discretionary dollars be allocated per needs verified by data ▪ Examine negotiated agreements for flexibility or waivers ▪ Reschedule student time consistent with transportation obligations
Modify time	▪ Uniform class periods ▪ Graduation requirements that limit opportunity to demonstrate proficiency in core standards ▪ Required time allotments in policy	▪ Construct dual classes for those in need ▪ Count dual courses in core competencies (math, English/reading, language arts/writing, science) ▪ Integrate content areas for instructional purposes
Modify opportunities	▪ Textbook-driven instruction ▪ Seat-time requirements for credits ▪ Limited course offerings or great variation in courses for same graduation requirement ▪ Prerequisites	▪ Collaboratively identify power standards ▪ Use standards-based grading ▪ Allow proficiency on standards to meet requirements for graduation ▪ Establish an opt-in provision for honors/IB/AP ▪ Change policies to open electives to all
Provide corrective feedback	▪ Fear or observation of retribution for speaking one's mind ▪ Culture of collegiality rather than collaboration ▪ Expectation of exemplary performance in all evaluations ▪ Candor viewed as threatening, inviting of grievances	▪ Establish operating norms for all teams that value candor, collaboration, diversity of ideas, corrective feedback ▪ Require data to support positions, recommendations ▪ Role-play format for team thinking ▪ Institute dialogue with association to set guidelines
Replicate successful practices	▪ Watered-down replication ▪ Path of least resistance ▪ Underestimation of training required ▪ Competing priorities that should be subtracted ▪ Push-back from unspoken and unwritten cultural expectations	▪ Replicate only when data warrants ▪ Provide in-depth training and modeling, and monitor quality indicators ▪ Consider context of replication in terms of work habits and processes, and identify what will be subtracted before adding anything new ▪ Establish clear norms for replication/innovation

Exhibit 1.9	

Barriers to the Ten Acts of Accountability (Continued)

Act of Accountability	Barriers	Remedies
Make midcourse corrections	■ Unrealistic curriculum coverage expectations ■ Single means to proficiency, such as written final exam ■ Grade expectations not based on standards ■ Traditions	■ Align curriculum and instruction to standards ■ Identify power standards that prioritize content ■ Develop scoring guides with multiple paths to proficiency ■ Align grades to standards ■ Gather data to verify traditional practices
Analyze diverse types of data	■ Existing data limited to student achievement ■ Teacher isolation and limited discussion of teaching strategies ■ Ignorance of power of classroom practices ■ Data examined annually; rearview-mirror effect prevails	■ Award staff development in data analysis with privileged choices to those who justify requests with diverse data ■ Have data teams examine and respond to actual student work ■ Discuss local strategies and expect that staff will become fluent with effective teaching strategies ■ Create structures to examine data routinely, at least twice per month
Collaboratively create, implement, and evaluate common assessments	■ Assessments limited to district requirements ■ Lack of common planning time ■ Professional development days committed to outside seminars, unrelated to local needs driven by data ■ Reluctance to accept collective wisdom of peers for individual classroom application	■ Create collaboration, common planning, early release times ■ Introduce collaboration at every faculty meeting ■ Align professional development to NCSD standards, student achievement gaps, and faculty needs to improve achievement ■ Build data system for teaching, curriculum, leadership, and a variety of student result measures ■ Train in group processes
Tailor training to needs	■ Optional training unrelated to vision, goals, student needs ■ Training unrelated to evaluation process ■ Data rarely disaggregated by antecedent strategies, structures, or teacher behaviors	■ Establish collaborative professional development ■ Have teachers teach teachers ■ Review context/integration: curriculum, standards, leadership ■ Attend to individual needs ■ Sustain and monitor internally
Develop and test hypotheses	■ Lack of incentives to innovate ■ Reliance on path of least resistance ■ No format for action research ■ Opinions and private information not valued	■ Use data system that promotes pursuit of hunches ■ Give access to simplified action research ■ Allow structured reflection time ■ Recognize and value risk taking and private information in written norms or policies

ineffective practices, educators do not have the tools they need to put accountability into action.

REARVIEW-MIRROR EFFECT

The *rearview-mirror effect* is defined simply as planning the future on the basis of events past. The analogy of driving by looking out the rearview mirror illustrates the challenge all too clearly. One does not consider what is ahead when looking out the rearview mirror, and anyone who does drive this way for more than a split second is inviting disaster, even on the quietest country road.

The rearview-mirror effect has four debilitating characteristics. The first is responding to a changing reality based on past events. A common example is educators waiting for instructional practices to be verified in the educational literature before allowing changes to be introduced. Schools often write improvement goals such as, "Eighty percent of students will demonstrate one or more years' growth on the state assessment or standardized achievement test." Measurable? Yes. Realistic? Probably. Helpful? No way. This goal effectively defines success as one student in five falling further and further behind! Rather than closing the learning gap, this plan accepts a wider opening.

Second, reliance on state assessment results as the single most important dimension of learning creates a high-risk environment, because data is examined after the fact. Annual assessments can be valuable in analysis, but reliance on annual assessments is part of the pernicious rearview-mirror effect because it creates a situation in which any response to the data is too little and too late. The most detailed school improvement plans periodically err in this way, glancing through a rearview mirror of data.

The third characteristic of the rearview-mirror effect is its focus on a single dimension of the highway, that is, a focus just on what students do. That is why it is so important to focus on the data of teaching, learning, improving, and persuading, and to examine everything that can influence the learning environment. Student achievement remains the essential focus of a data management system, but the data will be collected purposefully to add value. Data is not just numbers, and examining only student achievement data is a recipe for frustration.

The fourth characteristic of the rearview-mirror effect is nostalgia, a wistful looking back to a prior time when things were simpler. Criticisms abound about the unfairness of state assessments. "If only I were left alone, I could go back to teaching." I am not criticizing the frustration the most dedicated teachers experience in high-stakes testing environments. I *am* pointing out that looking back, whether by the superintendent, classroom teacher, parent, or board member, is counterproductive. It is akin to driving via the rearview mirror, with all the attendant consequences. Sustained, breakthrough improvements in student achievement that outperform expectations will never occur if those responsible for creating them look to the past for tomorrow's answers. Instead, let's briefly turn to another approach to monitoring student achievement.

CANARIES IN THE COAL MINE

Canaries were used for centuries as an early warning signal of gas leaks and accumulations in underground mines. If the canaries stopped singing, or keeled over, miners knew it was time to get out—and get out fast! The rearview-mirror effect will continue to plague educators until they and their schools develop their own "canaries in the coal mine." What "canaries" will allow schools and teachers to make adjustments quickly and respond with agility based on student needs? Routine, corrective, and instructive feedback assists teachers to make adjustments almost immediately, but one structure in particular holds considerable promise as a "canary" in each classroom.

Data Teams

Data teams are collaborative, structured, scheduled team meetings that focus on teaching and learning (Center for Performance Assessment, 2004). Teams may be entire faculties, but are more apt to be small grade-level or department teams that examine individual student work and analyze antecedent data—not just down to the classroom level, but to the individual student. Teachers bring specific student data to each meeting; this is a powerful strategy because a persistent problem for one student is frequently very similar to that experienced by several others. By assisting a colleague to address the problem identified, teachers help themselves address the needs of many students. Data teams adhere to continuous improvement cycles, examine patterns and trends, and establish specific timelines, roles, and responsibilities to facilitate analysis that results in action. Exhibit 1.10 combines the well-known strengths, weaknesses, opportunities, and threats (SWOT) framework for analysis with the data team emphasis on student performance and evidence of teaching as a means to gather critical data for your first data team meeting. (A template is provided in Appendix F.)

Effective data teams are "canaries in the coal mine" because of the frequency of meetings, use of mini-lessons, and focus on actual students with names and faces. This tool engages teams to take collective responsibility for student achievement results; communicates simple, clear, and useful meeting guidelines; and provides a proven process for improvement. The Center for Performance Assessment's "Data Team" seminar (CPA, 2004) provides an excellent three-meeting format, in which each meeting has a distinct, identified purpose: before making instructional modifications; during the instructional intervention and period of data gathering; and following intervention, to review the success of any changes made. This cycle typically occurs in twice-monthly meetings, meaning that the goals and interventions are implemented and reviewed within four to five weeks. This is a clear illustration of monitoring that minimizes the rearview-mirror effect. A comparison of actions that produce change and facilitate improved student achievement with the average referral process for students at risk often reveals that data teams respond faster and more effectively than traditional referral efforts.

Exhibit 1.10

SWOT Analysis for Data Teams

	Strengths	Weaknesses	Opportunities	Threats
Student performance	Students grasp concept of biosphere per quizzes 85%+ Classification, vocabulary demonstrated	Unit test failure, 62% average Problem solving, inventing, and determining cause/effect relationships re biosphere Weak performance on extended response assessments Has yet to demonstrate writing with problem-solving strategies	Projects that call for higher-level operations re Bloom's taxonomy Explicit problem-solving strategies More writing opportunities Unit lends itself to wide range of activities and projects	Time is limited before state assessment (90 days) Sense of efficacy is weak History of poor academic performance Struggles with activity transitions Easily distracted by noise, social opportunity
Evidence of teaching	Ticket-out-the-door writing activity (daily) Characteristics, types of living organisms, and interaction in biospheres introduced with vocabulary	Essential questions and planned transitions not observed Questioning is primarily single response (yes-no, true-false)	Introduce unit and essential questions Establish cooperative learning groups Use Cornell Notes to summarize daily lessons Use open-ended questions	Number of students at risk in classrooms Difficulty finding time to collaborate with and observe colleagues Training in Bloom's taxonomy not scheduled until next fall

SUMMARY

This chapter introduced the notion of proof by describing some characteristics associated with proof in several contexts. Educators who bristle at the requirements of the No Child Left Behind Act need to understand that the public, in this data-rich era, though supportive of teaching as a profession, have also accepted the notion of test scores as a measure of a school's effectiveness. Test scores on assessments that appear far removed from teaching and learning are also test scores that reflect mastery on standards developed in almost every state by teachers themselves. We are rapidly approaching a time when a sophisticated audience will demand external validation of effectiveness, and it behooves the profession to seize the opportunity to introduce compelling evidence—separate from the distant state assessments—that validates our craft and provides us with diagnostic information to leverage antecedents into sustained improvement for Tier 1 (state and district) data, Tier 2 (school) data, and Tier 3 (contextual and classroom) data.

This chapter introduced a three-part standard for proof: a compelling rationale based on a preponderance of all types of evidence; a means to satisfy the skeptics with data of teaching, learning, and improvement; and a persuasive argument that objectively explains external test data with a depth of knowledge of the antecedents that produce excellence and an open and transparent delineation of student achievement results. Seven practical tools of analysis were introduced, with practical examples of their use; templates for all these tools are included in the appendices to this book. A comprehensive scoring guide matrix, found in Appendix G, describes a continuum of skills and competencies in terms of antecedents of excellence, collaboration, and accountability.

Show Me the Proof! offers teachers, principals, and practitioners at all levels the tools to enlarge the universe of meaningful information (data); capture the data of teaching, learning, improving, and persuading; and apply numerous tools of accountability, antecedent management, and collaboration to make visible what is now invisible to us as professionals.

DISCUSSION

BIG IDEA

State assessments will continue to act as the primary indicator of effectiveness until educators find ways to demonstrate "proof" of effectiveness through the data of teaching, learning, improving, and persuading.

QUESTIONS

1. *Why is a compelling rationale insufficient to "show the proof" of learning?*

2. *Describe the difference between the data of teaching and the data of improving.*

3. *Of the seven tools presented in this chapter, which do you feel will be most useful in your setting? Why?*

Types of Data

*There are three kinds of lies: lies, damned lies,
and statistics.*

—Benjamin Disraeli (1804–1881)

Mr. Disraeli's comment, made in the nine-
teenth century, resonates today, in large part because data, numbers, and statistics are
often viewed as having little practical application to the craft of teaching. Unfortunately,
this common perception ignores the value of statistics to the practitioner. Statistics is
merely "the study of how to acquire meaningful information by analyzing data" (Downing & Clark, 1997, viii), and few practitioners need a Ph.D. in statistics to become
experts in data analysis. *Data* is the raw material of information that must be translated
into meaning. Although life offers many things of beauty and wonder that we wouldn't
even want to try to reduce to data, most data can yield insights we would not gain without analysis of that data.

Consider the limits of the English language when compared to the nuances of the
Greek, with its multiple definitions and distinctions of the word *love*. The translation
is of great value to our understanding. In the same way, statistics is like the universal
serial bus (USB) that allows us to "plug and play" across computer platforms, across
devices, and across contexts. Though the analogy is limited, it helps describe the common
language and capacity that statistics provides across disciplines. Educators who understand the distinctions among types of data are better able to apply the full range of possibilities in their analyses to improve student achievement.

We spend enough time collecting data. We should afford ourselves a similar opportunity to understand and apply it. School leaders and teachers are the most capable of
selecting data that measures improvement or teaching, learning or provides evidence
that persuades. This chapter describes data in terms of what we might do with it. We
examine both the data of statistical analysis and data categorized by the purpose for
which the data is collected.

TYPES OF DATA BY THE NUMBERS

Data is typically defined in terms of its properties or characteristics, such as its potential for statistical analysis. We could classify objects in terms of colors or shapes rather
than numbers, but our capacity to analyze numbers is much greater. Like USB connectors, we use them because of their universal applicability. Hence, data is defined in
terms of levels of measurement, nominal data, dichotomous data, ordinal data, interval
data, and ratio data. Data is also defined in terms of its distribution and our ability to
test it for significance, so this section briefly reviews the properties of parametric and
nonparametric data. The following abbreviated definitions provide the basis of and
starting point for statistical analysis.

Nominal Data

Data is *nominal* when it distinguishes one group from another. Nominal data merely
classifies in such a way that members in the group have a common set of characteristics and members can be in only one category. Green eyes, brown hair, the wealthy, those
in poverty, citizens of Canada: these are all nominal forms of data, as are the subgroups
identified for NCLB purposes. Fifty-three bananas and fourteen tomatoes represent
nominal data. You are in or out.

Dichotomous data is a form of nominal data that not only identifies groups and
individuals, but also represents pairs of data that are incompatible with each other:
male/female, true/false, yes/no, tall/short. Analysis of dichotomous data will reveal more
information than analysis of nominal data, but less than analysis of ordinal data.

Ordinal Data

Data that is *ordinal* offers greater opportunity for analysis because it not only classifies
subjects (as does nominal data) but also ranks them in terms of the degree to which a
characteristic is present. Rank in a graduating class; ranking in terms of tallest to short-
est; and gold, silver, and bronze Olympic medals are ordinal data. Percentile rank is also
ordinal data. However, the ninety-eighth percentile and the ninety-seventh may differ
by only one item, whereas the difference between the forty-sixth and forty-fifth percentile may be eighteen items. Percentile scores represent rankings only. The gold-medal
winner and the silver-medal winner may be separated by a fraction, but only one person
won the gold and another the silver. Ordinal data ranks, all right, but it does not provide
information about what separates groups or individuals. Ordinal data can be analyzed
with more clarity than nominal data, but yields less information than interval data.

Interval Data

Data that is *interval* possesses the same characteristics as nominal and ordinal data,
but also has an equal distance between each score; that is, the scores or rankings fall at

equal intervals. Raw scores represent the number of items passed on a state assessment. Height in centimeters and weight in pounds are interval data. The difference between a score of 351 and a score of 496 is the same as the difference between 496 and 641: 145 items. Interval data does not have a true zero (this explains why we cannot assume that one diver's score of 9.0 means twice as good a dive as the diver who received a 4.5 on the same type of dive).

The scientist's ideal data scale is *ratio*. It meets the tests for nominal, ordinal, and interval data, and it has a true zero point that allows one to confidently make mathematical inferences and predictions about relationships and variations.

STATISTICAL SIGNIFICANCE

Significance merely means that the results of the study indicate that the relationship or difference between the variables studied is of such a magnitude as to rule out its happening by chance (Downing & Clark, 1997, 302). This does not mean that the differences are always important—only that the findings cannot be ruled out on the basis of chance. Statistical analysis is all about rejecting or accepting the null hypothesis.

Null Hypothesis

The null hypothesis concept states that there will be no relationship (or difference) between the variables studied, and that any relationship found will be a chance relationship, not a true one. All statistical tests are designed to allow the researcher to make this critical determination before answering the question, "So what?" The null hypothesis is the starting point for digging deeper. Let us now turn to the two primary types of statistical tests for significance.

Parametric Data

Parametric data includes all interval and ratio data because they meet the three criteria required for parametric tests of significance:

1. The item measured (*variable*) is one for which the population is normally distributed.
2. The data represents an interval or ratio scale of measurement.
3. Subjects are selected independently for the test.

The third criterion is really an assumption that selection of participants will be random and representative. The first criterion assumes that the population of the group represents the same distribution as the population; that is, it is assumed that more than two-thirds of the population will score within one standard deviation of the mean, and more than 95 percent will score within two standard deviations of the mean. In essence, parametric data anticipates and assumes that reality is reflected in a bell-curve-shaped distribution.

Use of Parametric and Nonparametric Data

Nonparametric data does not depend on any assumptions of normality. Nonparametric data is nominal, dichotomous, and ordinal data, rather than interval or ratio data. Nonparametric tests determine significance not by variance, correlation, or regression, as is the case with parametric data, but rather by a few properties that can be tested against a chance expectation. Because much nonparametric data is dichotomous, a single property can be tested against chance expectation. When the null hypothesis of chance is rejected, one can assume from the nonparametric test that differences are significant. Other properties used to calculate departures from chance include the range of responses, distribution, and rank order (Kerlinger, 1986, 274). Nonparametric tests of significance examine these properties to determine significant differences that cannot be attributed to chance.

Researchers are in agreement about parametric and nonparametric data, and also agree on the integrity of parametric and nonparametric tests of significance, but debate whether certain forms of data should utilize a parametric or nonparametric test. A general rule of thumb is:

> *When you are unsure whether the*
> *assumptions for parametric data have been met,*
> *use a nonparametric test.*

These categories and definitions are important in applying basic statistical tests of significance. Several parametric and nonparametric tests of significance are defined in the glossary.

DATA ON PURPOSE

The statistical basis provides a foundation for data analysis, but very few practitioners have the time, inclination, or background to perform tests of significance for their students or in the context of their teaching. It may be possible to periodically run *t* tests to compare groups, or chi-square tests to examine proportions, and educators often create scattergrams that can offer a Pearson's *r* to determine significance. Such efforts can serve to validate current practices or suggest a different direction, but educators must get out in front in terms of managing the dynamics of teaching and learning, and statistics seldom govern educational practice in the field. Clearly, a different approach is warranted. Schools need an approach that links the data to what we intend to do with it. The following framework describes data in terms of actions we want to effect, and uses four types of data: teaching, learning, improving, and persuading.

Some may argue that everything that transpires in schools should have a direct influence on teaching and learning. It is true that caring, skilled, and highly professional bus drivers and a fleet of vehicles that are well maintained and replaced on a ten-year schedule send a positive and welcoming message to students and families. They also are powerful indicators of safety, and my own experience has demonstrated that bus drivers may act as de facto teachers for students, influencing decisions to apply themselves, to stay in school, and even to choose a particular career. However, is the degree to which a bus fleet is maintained really about student achievement? Is safety primarily about student achievement? In fact, both these measures are very important indicators of effectiveness in our schools, and both demonstrate the degree to which adults in that system are committed to students. Nonetheless, these measures are more about improvement, providing data to help us do something better this month than we did last month. They are examples of the data of improvement.

Each of the four types of data allows greater precision in planning and application when we address the purpose for which the data is collected. The distinctions also help practitioners identify the data associated with the actions of teaching, the data associated with the actions of learning, the work habits that continue over time but invite improvement, and the forms of data that are most persuasive for changing practices and policies and redirecting resources.

There is an ulterior motive for defining data by its purpose. When we describe data in terms of the *acts* of teaching, learning, improving, and persuading, it is hard to escape or ignore the need to take some action based on the lessons learned from the data. Educators who are intent on having the capacity to make informed decisions on the basis of data will agree: *action must follow analysis*. We can modify teaching and learning conditions, and we can improve the quality of our implementation, routines, and work habits. If we are cognizant of the types of data needed to persuade decision makers of the merits of our efforts, we will be more focused and ultimately, more effective. Exhibit 2.1 offers examples of data on purpose.

The Data of Teaching

To state the obvious, teaching has considerable influence on student achievement. In fact, the evidence in recent years has begun to replace the myth that poverty and race sentence students to low performance with an understanding that teaching practice has the greatest impact on student learning—more than resources and class size, more

Exhibit 2.1

Data Types by Purpose

Data of Teaching	Data of Learning
■ % of assessments that are performance assessments ■ % of common assessments designed, implemented, evaluated collaboratively ■ Instructional strategies applied to lesson planning to produce specific results ■ % of lessons with required writing ■ Frequency of corrective feedback disaggregated by students or content	■ % of time devoted to reading or writing ■ % of time working in groups ■ Extended-response problem solving ■ Self-assessment of performance ■ Measures of thinking, reasoning ■ Quantitative and qualitative measures of nonfiction writing in content areas

Data of Improving	Data of Persuading
■ Steps to introduce specific concepts ■ Process for subject transitions ■ Protocol for developing lesson plans ■ Steps for creating a master schedule ■ Process to align curriculum to standards ■ Routines to collaborate re student work ■ Process to establish learning groups ■ Schedule for implementing policies ■ Protocol for designing professional development on student achievement	■ Student achievement results ■ End-of-course (EOC) assessments ■ Relationship of professional development expenditures to student achievement results ■ Patterns and trends by cohort(s) ■ Budgets-to-actual expenditures ■ Relationship of antecedents to results by classrooms, schools ■ Action research results

than education level, and certainly more than family income (Wenglinsky, 2002; Sanders, 1998; Reeves, 2002, 75). The irony, then, is that educators and policy makers have focused almost exclusively on student achievement data and neglected the measures of what contributes most to student achievement: the data of teaching. Feedback, collaboration, use of performance assessments, and required writing are examples of the data of teaching. Only when that data is systematically gathered is it possible to determine the impact of such practices on student achievement. Exhibit 2.2 demonstrates how powerful the data of teaching can be in illuminating our understanding of student achievement results, and in deciding what to do about it.

Exhibit 2.2

The Data of Teaching in Action

Classroom	Students Scoring Proficient/Advanced	Corrective Feedback (days/week)	Common Assessments (per year)	Daily Writing (days/week)
A	54%	0	0	3
B	63%	3	2	4
C	72%	4	6	5

The example is perhaps simplistic in suggesting that student achievement is highly correlated with these three examples of the data of teaching, but the research is compelling for each of the antecedents utilized (Marzano, Pickering, & Pollock, 2001a; Schmoker, 1999; Reeves, 2002, 5). Increase the presence of these antecedents and you *will* see student achievement improve.

The Data of Learning

One might assume that student achievement data constitutes the data of learning, but the data of learning is really about other, more precise indicators of learning than test scores. Consider what kinds of things occur when students are learning. Robert Fulghum's famous book, *All I Really Need to Know I Learned in Kindergarten* (1989), identified profound learning that transpires in kindergarten classrooms every day: Share everything, play fair, say you're sorry when you hurt somebody. These are the data of learning, as are evidence of higher-order thinking and inquiry in classroom discussions, self-assessments, use of graphic organizers, Cornell note taking with reflective summaries, and other evidence of thinking. Yes, student achievement data may represent the result of thinking, engagement, and application, but if we identify measures of learning, we will expand the data available for decisions using more direct—and therefore more valid—measures than traditional test scores. Such assessments will be explicit, embedded, and standards-based.

"Unwrapping" of standards provides a very useful methodology for identifying all four types of data, and the process is instructive in distinguishing each type. Larry Ainsworth defines the "unwrapping" process as follows:

> "Unwrapping" the academic content standards is a *proven technique to help educators identify from the full text of the standards exactly what they need to teach their students.* "Unwrapped" standards provide clarity as to what students must know and be able to do. When teachers take time to **analyze** each standard and identify its **essential** concepts and skills, the result is more effective instructional planning, assessment, and student learning (2003, 1 [emphases added]).

Ainsworth goes on to detail a process of unwrapping whereby educators separate the skills of the standards from the concepts and content by identifying the words of action (verbs) as skills to be demonstrated, and by identifying the knowledge students must acquire to meet the standard (nouns and noun phrases). Teachers are then free to match the words of action to the concepts and content, in effect multiplying the opportunities for students to demonstrate their proficiency as to the standard.

By collaboratively reducing the skills and knowledge to a graphic organizer, educators are guided to see the myriad of possibilities for instruction and garner a much deeper, hands-on understanding of the standard itself. For example, fourth-grade science students might be asked to identify adaptations of living things, distinguish those adaptations, demonstrate adaptations in real life, explain them in a presentation, and evaluate them in terms of our responsibility for the natural world. All these actions address the same standard, meeting one acid test for a quality, standards-based assessment: multiple opportunities to achieve proficiency. Applied to data analysis, the unwrapping process offers multiple ways to monitor learning, teaching, improving, and persuading. By identifying key data points on the front end of data analysis, we avoid the rearview-mirror effect of "if only we had the data" when we examine achievement data after the fact.

Consider the actions selected from teacher-developed performance assessments in Exhibit 2.3. All 148 actions can be observed, measured, and monitored to determine influence on student achievement. For example, could we recognize performance when students **infer** from a literary text what the author was saying about life in general? Could we create a standard teachers could agree on regarding the ability to **factor** in the effect of population growth on our weather systems? I deliberately chose the more obscure actions to emphasize how each can be monitored to determine the degree to which the data of teaching, learning, improving, and persuading is related to student achievement. Physical activities were largely omitted so that we could concentrate on actions of thinking that can be observed and observed reliably if we are explicit in our descriptions and expectations.

Exhibit 2.3

Verbs: Actions of Measurement, Monitoring, and Proof

▪ Add	▪ Complete	▪ Determine	▪ Exchange
▪ Address	▪ Compose	▪ Differentiate	▪ Explain
▪ Align	▪ Comprehend	▪ Discover	▪ Explore
▪ Analyze	▪ Compute	▪ Discuss	▪ Express
▪ Answer	▪ Conclude	▪ Display	▪ Extend
▪ Anticipate	▪ Conduct	▪ Distinguish	▪ Facilitate
▪ Apply	▪ Connect	▪ Divide	▪ Factor
▪ Brainstorm	▪ Construct	▪ Draft	▪ Find
▪ Calculate	▪ Convert	▪ Draw	▪ Follow
▪ Categorize	▪ Convey	▪ Edit	▪ Formulate
▪ Challenge	▪ Create	▪ Elaborate	▪ Generate
▪ Check	▪ Debate	▪ Elevate	▪ Graph
▪ Cite	▪ Defend	▪ Employ	▪ Help
▪ Clarify	▪ Define	▪ Encourage	▪ Honor
▪ Classify	▪ Deliver	▪ Enlist	▪ Identify
▪ Collect	▪ Demonstrate	▪ Establish	▪ Illustrate
▪ Combine	▪ Depict	▪ Estimate	▪ Infer
▪ Communicate	▪ Derive	▪ Evaluate	▪ Integrate
▪ Compare	▪ Design	▪ Examine	▪ Interpret

Exhibit 2.3

Verbs: Actions of Measurement, Monitoring, and Proof (Continued)

▪ Improve	▪ Monitor	▪ Pursue	▪ Share
▪ Include	▪ Multiply	▪ Question	▪ Show
▪ Investigate	▪ Narrow	▪ Quiz	▪ Solve
▪ Judge	▪ Obtain	▪ Read	▪ Speak
▪ Justify	▪ Observe	▪ Recognize	▪ Study
▪ Know	▪ Organize	▪ Reduce	▪ Subtract
▪ Label	▪ Outline	▪ Refine	▪ Summarize
▪ Link	▪ Paraphrase	▪ Reflect	▪ Sustain
▪ List	▪ Participate	▪ Reinforce	▪ Synthesize
▪ Listen	▪ Perform	▪ Relate	▪ Tell
▪ Locate	▪ Persuade	▪ Research	▪ Trace
▪ Manipulate	▪ Plan	▪ Resolve	▪ Transcribe
▪ Maintain	▪ Predict	▪ Respond	▪ Understand
▪ Manage	▪ Process	▪ Reveal	▪ Utilize
▪ Match	▪ Produce	▪ Review	▪ Verify
▪ Measure	▪ Proofread	▪ Revise	▪ Validate
▪ Model	▪ Prove	▪ Save	▪ Work
▪ Modify	▪ Provide	▪ Select	▪ Write

Armed with this wealth of potential actions, describe the types of data in terms of what actions would be useful to monitor in your classroom or school. Associate just five actions to the data of teaching and learning. An example is provided in each section to start the process (see Exhibit 2.4).

Lists of actions that transpire in classrooms every day illustrate how readily available key data points are to the practitioner. When educators draw from these data points,

Exhibit 2.4

Potential Measures (Data) of Teaching and Learning

Data of Teaching	Data of Learning
Teachers *model* at least one effective teaching strategy at each faculty or team meeting.	Percent of class periods/week during which students *write* to *summarize* their understanding of nonfiction material in each discipline.
1.	1.
2.	2.
3.	3.
4.	4.

they become well equipped to make meaningful decisions about student achievement. Let us now apply the same approach to the data of improving and persuading in Exhibit 2.5.

Exhibit 2.5

Potential Measures (Data) of Improving and Persuading	
Data of Improving	**Data of Persuading**
1. *Create* a process map (flowchart) describing the steps needed to implement the 4-Block literacy framework.	1. *Compare* the relationship between attendance and achievement by creating a scattergram.
2. *Monitor* the number of intercom interruptions per week.	2. *Validate* the impact of activity participation on student achievement by comparing grades, EOC assessments, and attendance of activity vs. nonactivity students.
3.	
4.	3.
	4.

The rule of thumb is simply:

Actions that can be observed can be measured and monitored to influence achievement.

SUMMARY

The type of data determines the type of analysis we can validly perform and the capacity we have to draw inferences and make judgments that result in actions to improve the quality of teaching and learning. This chapter presented a compelling rationale to create data that adds value to the student achievement data we routinely examine. It's ironic that the more we pay attention to data other than traditional student achievement data, the more capable we are of influencing and improving student achievement. The evidence is clear that teachers and teacher leaders have a profound influence on that achievement. To identify and understand the antecedents that lead to excellence in student achievement, we must be able to gather a preponderance of evidence about teaching, learning, and improving.

There is value in understanding the distinctions among the types of data for statistical purposes, but there is greater value in recognizing the data of learning that should be monitored, or the data of improving so that we can make the most of our limited resources. The next chapter introduces six powerful methods of analysis, methods not unlike the types of data described here. Both chapters allow us to participate fully in *analysis,* which one dictionary (Merriam-Webster, 2003, 44) defines as: "separation of a whole into its component parts."

DISCUSSION

BIG IDEA

If data is worth collecting, you should have a purpose for collecting it.

QUESTIONS

1. *The purpose of statistical tests is to allow us to draw inferences from the* _____ *to the* _____ .

2. *Describe the purpose of the following forms of data, using the following key:*
   A = Teaching   B = Learning   C = Improving   D = Persuading

   EOC assessments _____

   Awareness of student learning gaps by student and standard _____

   Steps in processing a requisition _____

   Cubing as a process to increase higher-order thinking _____
   (Adapted from Gregory & Chapman, 2002, 12–15.)

3. *What advantage do actions provide in selecting the right data to monitor?*

CHAPTER **3**

A Data Road Map

Water, water, everywhere
And all the boards did shrink;
Water, water, everywhere,
Nor any drop to drink . . . .
—SAMUEL TAYLOR COLERIDGE (1772–1834)
The Rime of the Ancient Mariner

$\mathbf{M}$r. Coleridge's famous rhyme illustrates a profound truth about plenty and want, and it is appropriate to include it in a study of data. Our dilemma is not that we are lacking in quantity of data. Rather, the dilemma in schools today is that educators lack a method to capture data, to make data work for teachers rather than dooming teachers and principals to labor mightily to conform to expectations about the data. This chapter provides a number of structures and strategies for monitoring existing school improvement plans, for ensuring that sufficient attention is given to the strategies and principles of effective data analysis, and for avoiding the trap of the rearview-mirror effect. The data road map discussed here plays on the metaphor of driving an automobile, and for good reason. Data-driven decision making has become an axiom in public education over the last decade. The data road map is designed to help educators get to their destination of improved student achievement, by supplying a framework that uses data to "drive" decisions more effectively than ever before.

INTERSECTIONS

A data road map is designed to reveal areas where improvement has been lacking or growth stagnant, and where efforts have failed to produce results. To address these issues head-on, the road map begins by considering the *intersections* of data: those places where our decisions will determine both our future direction and our safety while reaching our destination. The term "data intersections" was coined by Victoria Bernhardt

(2000, 34) in reference to the need to consider multiple data points in data analysis. Although she drew primarily from measures of student achievement and student participation, Dr. Bernhardt introduced a powerful concept of multiple data points that was much needed in data analysis. Holcomb (2004, 78) suggested that data be systematically subjected to triangulation, by introducing one subjective and two objective measures into every goal-setting discussion. Triangulation of data is critical if we are to meet the standard of proof set forth in Chapter 1.

In the data road map, the recommendation to practitioners as to the intersection of data is to examine the student achievement results from three perspectives: antecedents, collaboration, and accountability. If these data are introduced to assist in the examination of student achievement results, you will soon find that you are on the path to success and sustained improvement. Two examples follow (see Exhibit 3.1). *Drive carefully!*

Exhibit 3.1

Data Intersection Examples

Example I. Student achievement results: 5 of 25 students are proficient and advanced

1. **No evidence of proven teaching strategies** ☹
   Antecedents:

2. **Works independently; collaboration informal** ☹
   Collaboration:

3. **Only instructional feedback provided is in evaluation conferences with principal** ☹
   Accountability:

Remedy:
- Weekly observation of colleague; literacy coach of self ✔
- Collaborative scoring to begin weekly; results shared ✔
- Book study: *Making Standards Work* ✔

Data suggests that this teacher is all alone and unfamiliar with proven teaching strategies. He works on all content areas alone, reducing possible impact in terms of depth of understanding and preparation. Teaming with colleagues is neither required nor facilitated, and the teacher has little idea what is expected of him. By addressing antecedents with the book study, collaboration with scoring of assessments and weekly observations, and accountability to one another in the process, this teacher is on his way to delivering more focused instruction and monitoring progress for students and himself through these changes.

Remedies that add value: _____

_____

_____

Exhibit 3.1

Data Intersection Examples *(Continued)*

Example II. Student achievement results: A growing learning gap for boys

1. **Choices to write or read (boys read)**   ☹
   Antecedents:

2. **Cooperative groups; students choose roles. Girls record minutes in all groups; group grades**   ☹
   Collaboration:

3. **Quiz and worksheet grades trump assessments in total points available**   ☹
   Accountability:

Remedy:

- Required writing every day, every subject, every student   ✔

- Flexible grouping with role rotations to ensure that every boy takes a turn as recorder and every student receives own grade   ✔

- Eliminate points for worksheets, increase emphasis on achieving proficiency; differentiate homework to address specific skill deficits   ✔

Data suggests that boys have had the capacity to opt out of the thinking and reasoning that writing requires; cooperative groups are seriously flawed, again allowing boys to avoid the work of thinking and reasoning. The value placed on quizzes and worksheets clearly communicated that writing was not valued. Remedies align efforts with desired results; removal of points for worksheets communicates importance of *learning*, not just completing work. Differentiation of homework will help close the gap.

Remedies that add value: _____

_____

Both of these examples revealed areas of concern by identifying antecedents (or a lack of them) in terms of effective teaching strategies. Both examples identified weaknesses in collaboration: in the first example, among adults; in the second example, in the collaborative structures created for students. In both examples, accountability was lacking, as to responsibility for results and as to the authority teachers exercised in the classroom.

Appendix H includes templates for each component of the data road map. The ability to triangulate data, to increase our understanding and our capacity to respond with insight and excellence, is critical for data analysis, and will be addressed further in Chapter 5.

DATA DRIVING HABITS

Section two of the data road map addresses the habits of driving by data. It concerns those routines, procedures, and events that occur every day that can be improved. Many are never monitored or reduced to writing, either because the process appears to be very mundane or because "we've always done it this way." These routines are indeed our habits of work and, like all habits, take time to acquire and discipline to discard. Examine the following data to determine what work habits should be changed, increased, and/or improved. Take a risk and identify a work habit that should be created as you respond to the following scenario (using Exhibit 3.2). Templates are included in Appendix H.

Exhibit 3.2

Data Driving Habits

To Change	To Increase	To Improve	To Create

CASE STUDY: NEW TIRES

Angeles Elementary was converted into a magnet school six years ago to attract students to a very mature suburb where families had long ago seen their children, and in some cases, grandchildren, graduate. For years the faculty lounge had been designated as the teacher's safe place, and four principals later, no administrator was admitted there.

Ms. Corwin, who just started work as the school secretary, began to inquire why she had to re-register existing families every fall and why all student records were kept on five-by-seven cards that required her to hand-type every permanent record. Mr. Ortega, the new principal, inquired about faculty meetings, and was told by a veteran teacher that everyone really appreciated the once-a-month, short and to the point, thirty-minute meeting that had become the standard—and no more. He was even more surprised to find that the professional development and instructional materials budgets were divided so that each classroom teacher had $750 per year to spend as he or she wished. Early release every Wednesday had been instituted eleven years ago, and the teachers had been using that time for needed planning and correction of papers, which they did almost entirely individually, rarely in collaboration.

Student achievement continued to languish in the district's lower quartile, but the middle-class neighborhood was now definitely low-income. Mr. Ortega was locking the building after moving into his new office, and on his way to buy new tires when there was a knock at the door.

"Can we come in?" said a rather timid and obviously new teacher. Sarah was accompanied by Lizzie, Craig, and Stephanie. The teachers looked at one another.

"What can I do for you?" asked Mr. Ortega.

Craig spoke up, reluctantly. "Mr. Ortega, we love this school and want you to know we are behind you 100 percent regarding any changes you need to make. We know we need to move ahead, we just aren't sure how to do that." The others, energized by Craig's courage, began to compete to tell their stories. . . .

REARVIEW-MIRROR EFFECT

The third component of the data road map involves attention to the rearview-mirror effects of using annual achievement results from state assessments as the primary source of data, relying only on student achievement measures, and looking backward to times when accountability and results were not as important as they are today. This section identifies some proactive strategies that interrupt and reduce any rearview-mirror effect. Take a few moments here to identify strategies that will help your school, district, or classroom better prepare itself for the future. An example is provided in Exhibit 3.3 to start the ball rolling.

The example introduces the notion of classroom data that is addressed in small working teams (departments) throughout the school. These settings are safe places for candor, and an accountability factor is built in as all teachers learn to rely on each other to collectively help students. Rather than relying on state assessments and waiting anxiously for results, this school will soon have multiple teams that focus on current student work and modify instruction based on their own professional expertise and insights, rather than methods or techniques dictated from another level.

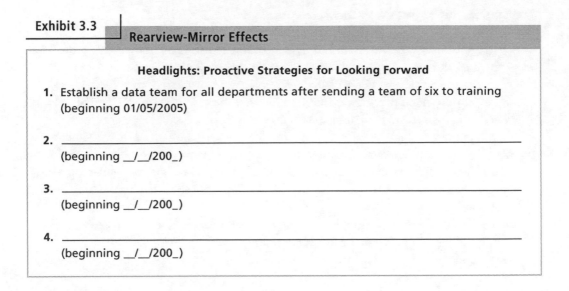

Exhibit 3.3

Rearview-Mirror Effects

Headlights: Proactive Strategies for Looking Forward

1. Establish a data team for all departments after sending a team of six to training (beginning 01/05/2005)

2. _____
   (beginning __/__/200_)

3. _____
   (beginning __/__/200_)

4. _____
   (beginning __/__/200_)

CANARIES FOR YOUR CLASSROOM

The fourth component of the data road map is the identification and use of early warning indicators—"canaries in the classroom"—to assist in creating formative assessments and interim data points that promote insightful midcourse modifications of instruction, curriculum, and work habits. For centuries, miners used canaries to warn of gas leaks. In this century, schools and classrooms need their own early warning indicators so that they can respond to the needs of students as those needs arise. Again, an example is provided in Exhibit 3.4. Use the blank spaces to identify "canaries" for your classroom or school. Appendix H contains a detailed template for this component.

All three early warning signals are designed to effect a cultural change. Examine the first classroom "canary," which states that students will leave class each day only after responding in writing to the classic KWL statements:

- What do I **K**now about the topic?
- What do I **W**ant to learn about the topic?
- How will I know I **L**earned it?

With student responses on three-by-five cards, the teacher will be able to examine writing skills and identify where students are in terms of the lesson of the day. To manage the process, teachers could address the outliers each day, or even examine feedback at random, being careful to provide feedback to every student every week. Keeping them guessing has always been a great motivator for quality work!

The "canary" at the school level is a *progress report,* a common method that has been employed to increase communication with parents, send a message of accountability home with students, and focus efforts away from grades and traditional assessments

Exhibit 3.4

Early Warning Indicators (Canaries)

Canaries for Your Classroom

1. KWL ticket out the door every day; every subject and class monitored weekly
   (beginning 09/03/2005)

2. _____
   (beginning __/__/200_)

3. _____
   (beginning __/__/200_)

4. _____
   (beginning __/__/200_)

Canaries for Your School

1. Institute progress reports that indicate progress by standard distributed every three weeks
   (beginning 4/15/2005)

2. _____
   (beginning __/__/200_)

3. _____
   (beginning __/__/200_)

4. _____
   (beginning __/__/200_)

Canaries for Your District

1. Every school will submit top performance assessment to be displayed quarterly in the board room
   (beginning 01/10/2005)

2. _____
   (beginning __/__/200_)

3. _____
   (beginning __/__/200_)

4. _____
   (beginning __/__/200_)

toward standards and achievement of proficiency. The three-week cycle enables schools to identify students who are falling behind by structuring time to examine progress reports and develop a rapid-response team for students at risk of growing learning gaps.

At the district level, the recommended "canary" is much more subtle, but the accountability factor of showcasing the best work every quarter in the board room will not only recognize students for excellence, but also demonstrate, once again, a focus on standards. I doubt very much if schools will be satisfied with showcasing the work of the same few teachers and high-performing students each month; thus, this "canary" creates an incentive to institutionalize the practice of doing performance assessments at high levels in every department and at every grade.

TRAFFIC SIGNALS AND SIGNS

The fifth component of the data road map addresses traffic signals, those signs that direct us on our journey. Feedback should be as ubiquitous as traffic lights.

Complete this section (see Exhibit 3.5) based on your own work setting, focusing on methods of receiving and responding to feedback that will improve curriculum, instruction, and overall school operations. Research shows very clearly that corrective, accurate, and timely feedback promotes excellence for both students and adults (Reeves 2002, 59; Marzano, Pickering, & Pollock, 2001a, 96).

Exhibit 3.5

Traffic Signals and Signs (Feedback Systems)

To Change	To Increase	To Improve	To Create
By __/__/200_	By __/__/200_	By __/__/200_	By __/__/200_

DETOURS AND ROAD CLOSURES

Step six is a very critical juncture for data analysis. Just as detours and road closures lengthen the journey and introduce potential problems, so do obsolete practices and policies. Does your work situation retain any obsolete practices? Programs? Antiquated and counterproductive organizational structures? Take your time to get rid of detours and road closures. It will save you more than time down the road. Exhibit 3.6 shows a sample worksheet for this area.

Exhibit 3.6

Detours and Road Closures

Practices to Subtract	Policies to Subtract	Programs/Organizational Structures to Subtract
Duplicated hand-delivered lunch count replaced by desktop entry by teachers	Site-based management policy that requires 80% faculty buy-in before any changes in curriculum are made, even though two schools are on AYP improvement level for failure to close the gap	Management-by-objective report instituted in 1973 requires eight hours per school to complete
By __/__/200_	By __/__/200_	By __/__/200_

USE YOUR DIGITAL CAMERA

Step seven of the data road map refers to the selection of results indicators that are easy to collect and very cost-effective in terms of time and effort expended. Sometimes we are our own worst enemies, as we attempt to create elaborate and complex systems for the sake of being thorough. Any data that requires more time to collect and analyze than is expended to make recommendations, decide, and implement changes is very expensive. Indicators, after all, are probes, snapshots. Volumes are for another business; educators are far too busy and our work far too important to add unnecessarily to the mountains of paper and forms that characterize so many schools and school districts. Like a digital camera, capture the moment, not the hour. Examples are provided for discussion purposes (see Exhibit 3.7).

Exhibit 3.7

Use Your Digital Camera (User-Friendly Embedded Data)

Snapshot Data— Students	Frequency	Snapshot Data— Adults	Frequency
Student-initiated self-assessments	Reported weekly at grade level or department meetings	Lessons created in collaboration with peers	Titles of lessons submitted to principal quarterly
Snapshot Data— Administrative Structures	**Frequency**	**Snapshot Data— Time and Opportunity**	**Frequency**
Monitor intercom interruptions	Monthly	Number of embedded integrated assessments that address standards in two or more disciplines	Departments report to principal quarterly

DATA IN ACTION

Component eight of the data road map addresses the data of teaching, learning, improving, and persuading—concepts introduced in previous chapters. Potential changes that monitor each area are suggested for your consideration (Exhibit 3.8). Reflect on changes you might institute to make your data management system more responsive to teaching and learning, improving and persuading.

Exhibit 3.8

Data in Action

Explicit Changes in Our DDDM System (collection, communication, calendar)

The Data of Teaching: What Adults Do

To Change	To Increase/Decrease	To Improve	To Create
Reduce proportion of time given to teacher-directed work and increase proportion given to student-directed work	Decrease lag time between submission of assignments and feedback/return of graded work	Lesson management by identifying standards and strategies to employ each lesson	Post essential questions for every unit that lead students to discover "Big Idea"
By __/__/200_	By __/__/200_	By __/__/200_	By __/__/200_

Exhibit 3.8

Data in Action *(Continued)*

The Data of Learning: Evidence of Thinking (Bloom's Taxonomy)

To Change	To Increase/Decrease	To Improve	To Create
Replace worksheets with KWL narratives	Increase frequency of higher-order and open-ended questions during instruction and in assessments	Use graphic organizers for discovery rather than facts and knowledge of contents	Process that rewards student reflection and self-assessment
By __/__/200_	By __/__/200_	By __/__/200_	By __/__/200_

The Data of Improving: Doing What We Do Now, Only Better

To Change	To Increase/Decrease	To Improve	To Create
Process for moving classroom formative grades from traditional A–F to standards-based rubrics of proficiency	Increase speed and quality (specificity and depth) of feedback to teachers regarding EOC assessments	The flow of student traffic in and out of the lunchroom	Process to get students help, on standards with which they are struggling, within 72 hours
By __/__/200_	By __/__/200_	By __/__/200_	By __/__/200_

The Data of Persuading

Trends to Establish	Patterns to Examine	Benchmarks to Achieve	Strengths to Celebrate
Performance by cohorts on the state assessments over time Proportion of budgets discretionary to leadership for improved performance over time Trends in closing the learning gap	Experience/training of teachers in relation to students from low-income homes Experience/training of teachers relating to students with learning gaps to standards Proportion of budgets given to professional development	All teachers certified in teaching areas, every school All schools meet or exceed AYP targets by 2010 All schools add one subgroup to meet or exceed AYP targets each year	Focused professional development rather than one-shot efforts Low rate of teacher turnover, high level of leader retention
By __/__/200_	By __/__/200_	By __/__/200_	By __/__/200_

This process is facilitated by inviting students to tell us what works. Research on engagement clearly highlights the value of inviting students to describe how their learning process could be improved (Fredricks, Blumenfeld, & Parks, 2004, 68; Sternberg, 2004, 5).

The final area of data management to be addressed is the data of persuading. This section refers both to the ethics of reporting data and to the need to create systems that make readily available persuasive data that aligns to mission and vision.

BUILDING YOUR SUPERHIGHWAY (LEADERSHIP)

The final step in using the data road map is to build capacity and future leadership by building a culture of team thinking, releasing authority to commit resources, and granting permission to stop doing things that are no longer needed. Examples are provided to start you thinking about how your leadership can affect your organization over the long term (Exhibit 3.9).

Exhibit 3.9

Building Your Superhighway (Leadership)

Strategies to Build Team Thinking	Strategies to Release Authority to Commit Resources	Strategies to Grant Permission to Stop
Establish operating norms for meetings; encourage role-playing to ensure that all sides of controversial issues are discussed and considered; train staff in listening skills and facilitation

Publicly recognize risk taking and thinking in new ways when action is aligned with stated and adopted mission of the organization | Develop sufficient processes to provide authority to commit resources within clearly defined limits prior to securing permission; build the structure down to the teacher level

Publicly recognize responsive action to serve students and their families

Emphasize rapid response and develop flowcharts for foreseeable contingencies, similar to crisis planning | Encourage integration of activities, wherever possible, with reward that subtracted event will not be replaced with a new one

Reward efforts to identify and reduce duplication of effort

Communicate and celebrate evidence of obsolete practices being subtracted

Invite creativity in combining functions

Flowchart all major processes to reveal unseen inefficiencies and duplication |

SUMMARY

Each component of the data road map is designed to assist educators to identify areas, in their current workplaces and across their organizations, that could be improved. The key to successful use of a data road map is to be explicit; the summary sheet in Exhibit 3.10 is designed to capture the efforts of each component with an implementation timeline.

Exhibit 3.10

The Data Road Map

Data Road Map

School: _____ School Year: _____

Data Team: _____

_____

Implementation Timeline

	Start	Evaluate	Complete
Intersections			
❑ Triangulation 1			
❑ Triangulation 2			
❑ Triangulation 3			
Data Driving Habits			
❑ To Change			
❑ To Increase			
❑ To Improve			
❑ To Create			
Rearview-Mirror Effect			
❑ Improve the Headlights			
❑ Canaries for the Classroom			
❑ Canaries for the School			
❑ Canaries for the System			
Traffic Signals and Signs			
❑ Feedback System Changes			
❑ Listening System Changes			
Detours and Road Closures			
❑ Practices to Subtract			
❑ Policies to Subtract			
❑ Structures to Subtract			

Exhibit 3.10

The Data Road Map *(Continued)*

Implementation Timeline *(Continued)*

	Start	Evaluate	Complete

Use Your Digital Camera:
Catch the Scenery

❑ Student Data

❑ Adult Data

❑ Structure Data

❑ Time and Opportunity Data

Data in Action

❑ Teaching

❑ Learning

❑ Improving

❑ Persuading

Building Your Superhighway
(Leadership)

❑ Team Thinking

❑ Agility in Committing Resources

❑ Permission to Stop

Summary: _____

_____

_____

_____

_____

_____

The data road map is a fun way of looking at the process of data analysis. Rather than yet another plan, for systems and schools already inundated with planning documents and required reports (that may even request contradictory data), the road map is a series of explicit strategies to make data management as efficient and effective as possible. Ordinary people accomplish extraordinary things when they make disciplined efforts to improve and are explicit in expectations, explicit in directives and timelines, explicit in communication, and explicit in monitoring efforts.

Whether it is the canaries in the classroom, that serve as early warning signals or probes of progress; or ways to eliminate the rearview-mirror effect; or ways to build leadership capacity, each component of the data road map is based on what we know works in schools and people-intensive organizations like schools. The intersections introduced you to the powerful practice of triangulation, and we offered two examples of how attention to collaboration, accountability, and antecedents in analyzing student achievement can both identify needs and point to solutions. Efforts to minimize the rearview-mirror effect, subtract obsolete practices and policies, and capture important but user-friendly data points with the digital camera are designed to help very good schools get even better. Chapter 4 introduces six powerful methods for analyzing data.

DISCUSSION

BIG IDEA

Incremental improvements change the ordinary into the extraordinary.

QUESTIONS

1. *Describe the component of the data road map that you anticipate will provide the greatest value to you and your organization. Why?*

2. *How can leadership build capacity by releasing the authority to commit resources to others?*

Methods for
Data Analysis

A little learning is a dangerous thing.
—ALEXANDER POPE (1688–1744)

Data without analysis is like standards without expectations. Most adults recognize that the most obvious explanation seldom tells the whole story, just as test scores fail to tell the real story behind the numbers. A hurried review of data, or failure to triangulate sufficiently to "hear" from the data, can easily create a cure that is worse than the disease. Because the way we look at data can determine whether we generate the answers we seek or the solutions we need, this chapter examines six data analysis methods. Trying to solve a problem when we really need to discover how things operate is a choice—and a mistake—that schools can ill afford.

The following methods apply to classroom, school, department, and school systems: systems analysis, solutions, decision making, clarification, action research, and continuous improvement. Extrapolated from forms of hypothesis generating and testing (Marzano, Pickering, & Pollock, 2001b), these methods approach data analysis from diverse perspectives. *Systems analysis* is used to bolster our understanding of a system's purpose, parts, and functions; it is a method of discovery. The *solutions* method is designed to generate answers, finding the most effective resolution to a challenge and achieving goals in spite of barriers. The *decisionmaking* analysis method is designed to help users choose from alternatives. *Clarification* analysis is a vehicle that provides specificity and clarity when we implement new programs; it helps align our efforts to our mission and vision. *Action research* analysis translates hunches from data into action in classrooms. *Continuous improvement* analysis strengthens daily routines and sustains innovation. The framework for this chapter is outlined in Exhibit 4.1.

As we examine each method, tools of analysis will be introduced with examples of data conundrums educators face every day. Like other aspects of data analysis, those serious about improving their management and application of data will find that changes

Exhibit 4.1   **Methods of Analysis**

Analysis Method	Purpose	Existing Data	Antecedents: Specific Behaviors, Strategies, Structures	Collaboration: Structures	Accountability: Structures
Systems Analysis	Clarify system purpose, parts, and functions: ■ Examine key subsystems in schools (7) ■ Reveal interdependence ■ Discover unintended consequences	■ Assessments of student achievement disaggregated ■ Technology data ■ Time/opportunity ■ Special ed numbers ■ Suspensions ■ Class assignments ■ Graduation requirements	Teaching strategies identified from research and by teacher teams to apply with specific students	■ Early release times ■ Department, data team meetings ■ Lesson logs ■ Common assessments ■ Instructional calendars	■ Frequent monitoring ■ Authority to act on data ■ Expectation that action will follow data analysis ■ Process for reporting to public ■ SMART measures
Solutions	Most effective resolution to achieve goals, given barriers, constraints	Allocation of time, schedules, contract terms, identified needs, subscale patterns, parent participation	■ Targeted student interventions/strategies ■ Use of new data tools (e.g., spider charts, relational diagrams, fishbones, 5 Ws, etc.)	■ Data teams ■ Improved strategies for communication ■ Reallocation of time and effort for reflection, collaboration	■ Frequent monitoring ■ Authority to act on data ■ Expectation that action will follow data analysis ■ Process for reporting to public ■ SMART measures
Decision Making	Choosing from alternatives: ■ Establishing criteria ■ Identifying alternatives ■ Weighted factors ■ Prioritization	Virtually all available data, including qualitative data	■ Staff trained in matrix for decision making ■ Facilitation skills ■ Operating norms (process, agree to hear all viewpoints, challenge assumptions, support final team decisions)	Teams: faculty, departments, data teams, grade-level teams, content-area teams, leverage teams (inter-disciplinary, horizontal, vertical teams), stakeholder teams	■ Frequent monitoring ■ Authority to act on data ■ Expectation that action will follow data analysis ■ Process for reporting to public ■ SMART measures

Analysis Method	Purpose	Existing Data	Antecedents: Specific Behaviors, Strategies, Structures	Collaboration: Structures	Accountability: Structures
Clarification	■ Clarify best practices ■ Apply lessons of research locally ■ Focus, align efforts to goal	■ Newly introduced strategies, programs, best practices ■ Controversial practices, traditions ■ Obsolescence, duplicated effort	■ Professional development plans ■ Range of choices ■ Timelines, incentives for training and implementation ■ Strategies to reward achievement and reinforce effort	■ Focus groups ■ Informal leader ■ Public support by leaders for innovation, best practices, strategies, training ■ Task force efforts ■ Parameters for research, clarification	■ Frequent monitoring ■ Authority to act on data ■ Expectation that action will follow data analysis ■ Process for reporting to public ■ SMART measures
Action Research	■ Translates hunches from data patterns to hypotheses and research in schools and classrooms ■ Applies findings from a data road map ■ Undertakes a proactive hunt for a better way	■ Triangulate with environmental scan data ■ Urgent data for improvements (i.e., AYP) ■ Replicable local practices data ■ Needs from gap analysis data	■ Standards-based classrooms in every school ■ Six steps of experimental inquiry commonly used by data and department teams ■ Faculty fluent in seven-step DDDM process ■ Student information systems conducive to standards-based assessments and reports	■ Data teams differentiate effective teaching strategies to meet needs of all students ■ Leadership teams fluent in seven steps of DDDM ■ Leverage teams fluent in power standards and performance assessments ■ Teams exist that analyze experimental inquiry data and draw inferences, conclusions, applications	■ Frequent monitoring ■ Authority to act on data ■ Expectation that action will follow data analysis ■ Process for reporting to public ■ SMART measures
Continuous Improvement	Framework to improve daily routines and sustained innovation at all levels for improved student achievement	■ All procedures ■ All flowchart processes ■ Data tracking time from plan to implementation ■ Data monitoring compliance at all levels	■ Faculty well trained in tools for invention: — Relations diagram — Seven-step DDDM — Affinity diagram ■ Uniform improvement procedures at all levels ■ Subtraction practiced with all extraneous data	■ Planned subtraction of announcements, useless data at faculty meetings ■ All team members proactively analyze data for discussion in advance ■ Team processes routinely identify improvements ■ Suggested improvements are recognized and rewarded	■ Frequent monitoring ■ Authority to act on data ■ Expectation that action will follow data analysis ■ Major processes reduced to writing and monitored ■ User-friendly timelines ■ Process for reporting to public ■ SMART measures

in this arena press for and drive changes in other areas as well. We should not be surprised at this, as data, like technology, is a form of communication that can add value to every aspect of educational systems. We begin, then, with systems analysis.

SYSTEMS ANALYSIS

Systemic reform, system-wide impact, restructuring, systems thinking, and systems analysis characterize much of the work of leading scholars in education today (Darling-Hammond, 1997; Evans, 1996; Fullan, 2001; Reeves, 2004a, 57–64; Schlechty, 2001; Senge, 2000). Peter Senge defines systems as "any perceived whole whose elements 'hang together' because they continually affect each other over time" (2000, 78). To Senge, systems need not be labeled as systems, nor are they even intended to exist. For the purpose of data analysis, we define systems in terms of five actions of discovery. Collectively, they provide us information (data) that looks beyond the obvious and helps us make visible those insights and understandings that would otherwise be invisible to us. *Systems analysis,* then, is:

1. Clarifying the purpose, parts, and function of a system
2. Examining key components of systems
3. Revealing interdependence
4. Discovering unintended consequences
5. Designing a process to monitor the health of the system

The first tool we will examine is the simple *flowchart* or process map, using an example showing how field trips and the instructional process are interdependent. Notice that Exhibit 4.2 also clarifies the connections among these areas. Ovals or circles indicate beginning or ending points, diamonds decisions or choices made, and rectangles steps or activities in the process.

The flowchart example clarifies the purpose, examines the key components and participants, and reveals the level of interdependence in the system. Can you identify possible unintended consequences from this scenario? Flowcharts supply a visual reference that is useful in considering the issues of systems analysis. Appendix J contains a template for two types of flowcharts or process maps.

The next systems analysis tool is the *environmental scan,* which examines seven key elements of any system: leadership, planning strategies, listening systems, information and data, work environment, work habits, and results (both performance and process results). Each of these areas is a system within a system, and the environmental scan examines programmatic, instructional, and organizational challenges for each system. One can see how the school or system that conducts a thorough environmental scan thereby monitors key factors to sustain successes and address current and emerging challenges. Environmental scans promote healthy organizations.

Exhibit 4.2 Flowchart Example: Guidelines for Field Trips and Standards-Based Instruction

Purpose: Field trips are an integral part of a comprehensive curriculum, providing the opportunity for hands-on application and extending the impact of teaching and learning beyond the four walls of the classroom. They offer powerful learning opportunities and motivate students to achieve new levels of performance and quality of work.

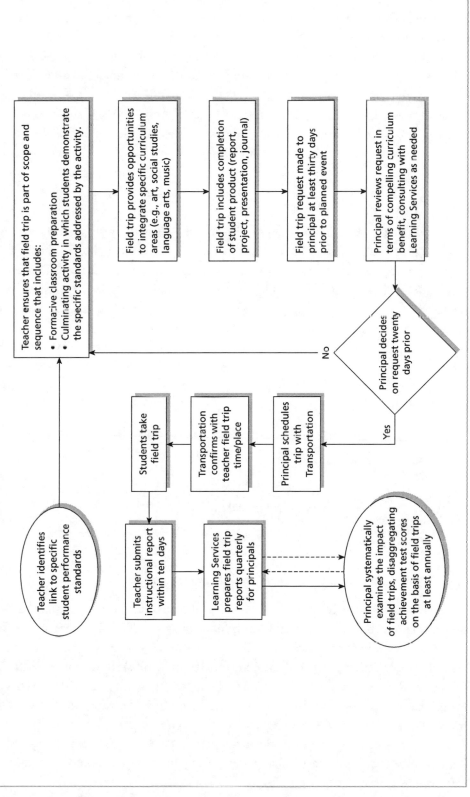

Teacher identifies link to specific student performance standards

Teacher ensures that field trip is part of scope and sequence that includes:
- Formative classroom preparation
- Culminating activity in which students demonstrate the specific standards addressed by the activity.

Field trip provides opportunities to integrate specific curriculum areas (e.g., art, social studies, language arts, music)

Field trip includes completion of student product (report, project, presentation, journal)

Field trip request made to principal at least thirty days prior to planned event

Principal reviews request in terms of compelling curriculum benefit, consulting with Learning Services as needed

Principal decides on request twenty days prior

No

Yes

Principal schedules trip with Transportation

Transportation confirms with teacher field trip time/place

Students take field trip

Teacher submits instructional report within ten days

Learning Services prepares field trip reports quarterly for principals

Principal systematically examines the impact of field trips, disaggregating achievement test scores on the basis of field trips at least annually

53

Exhibit 4.3 shows a very detailed environmental scan to guide our discussion. In terms of leadership, the school system is looking at Reading Recovery's effectiveness, expectations regarding standards and assessments, and whether site-based management is accomplishing what it was intended to do. Note how all three of these issues are addressed in terms of what is known, what the analysts want to know, and the evidence they need to verify their learning. In the column "Work Habits," the scan shows that the issues facing the district include barriers to a high-quality professional development program, concern about time wasted beginning classes in every school, and the issue of duplication of effort and rising costs. The depth of analysis and breadth of challenges identified make the environmental scan one of the most powerful tools for systems analysis.

Let us turn to the second method of analysis, *solutions*. From Exhibit 4.1, we know that the purpose of this method is to find the most effective solution that will allow us to achieve our goals. To illustrate, we apply two powerful tools, the Hishakawa cause-and-effect Fishbone and force-field analysis. (Appendix Q provides a template for the cause/effect fishbone.) We will examine a hypothetical school that has been very successful at increasing student achievement at every grade. Other schools in the district have not fared so well, so our task is to glean from the experience of Woodside Elementary what works and apply it to a very problematic situation on the other side of town. The fishbone in Exhibit 4.4 is relatively complete, but before discussing the data itself, let us identify several tips to help us get the most out of these cause-and-effect analyses:

- Brainstorm for possible causes of the effect or problem
- Assign possible causes to basic categories
- Use responses to "why?" as branches to causes
- Look for causes that appear repeatedly
- Reach consensus
- Gather data to determine the relative impact of causes
- Develop an action plan to address cause at its root.

Now that we are equipped with strategies for future fishbone analyses, what can we glean from this data that will be helpful to the sister school, where success has been so elusive? In terms of people, the student demographics suggest a real challenge, but we also note very little turnover, focused efforts to increase skills and pursue further education, and a principal who is committed (fifth year) to the school and has very clear expectations. The sister school has established common planning, there are lots of classroom observations, and every faculty meeting is about professional development and modeling of strategies. It also undertook a very focused curriculum effort and directed Title 1 resources to improve achievement. Are you ready to make some suggestions to this sister school?

Exhibit 4.3 Environmental Scan for Data Analysis

	Leadership	Planning Strategies	Listening Systems	Information and Data	Work Environment	Work Habits	Results—Process and Performance
Programmatic	Reading Recovery	School Improvement Process (SIP)	Satisfaction surveys	Data—student achievement tracking	Negotiated work day/hours	Barriers to professional development to improve instruction	State assessment AYP, EOC requirements
Know (current knowledge)	1.0 FTE staff assigned to each school	Requirements, expectations, and deadlines	Data is inconclusive	Expectation to report results to community	Policies and terms of negotiated agreement	Programs, policies, and traditions	Trends and patterns with dates when subgroup gaps must be closed
Want (to know)	Program effectiveness?	Possibility of midyear changes and process to add antecedent data indicators?	What do students, parents, and teachers really think?	How to include qualitative data and antecedents to student achievement data?	How much latitude to accommodate with flexible hours, waivers, and compensation?	What is needed to align with standards, increase agility, and improve instruction?	Impact of investment in professional development, curriculum alignment with standards, and triangulation of data?
Learn (evidence)	% proficient in reading within six months discontinued —Cost-benefit $	Specific process for midcourse changes and use of antecedents	Creation of alternate data collection systems	Evidence of gaps in achievement closing, obsolete subtracted	Areas where principals can leverage incentives to achieve results	Specify policies, traditions, and barriers; actions needed when?	What is working? Actions to replicate practices that work and remove existing barriers
Instructional	Expectations re standards and assessments	Effective teaching strategies (ETS)	Student view of classroom instruction	Data—tracking of local practices to replicate	Ability-grouping, secondary; elementary departmentalization	Opening classroom activities	Cohort improvement by subgroup and gaps opening or closing

(continues)

Exhibit 4.3

Environmental Scan for Data Analysis *(Continued)*

	Leadership	Planning Strategies	Listening Systems	Information and Data	Work Environment	Work Habits	Results—Process and Performance
Know	Standards are aligned with daily lessons	Teachers employ one or more daily	Students have no means to register concerns	No system is in place currently	Wide variation; little training; no clear expectations	Wide variation; little training; no clear expectations	Three years of cohort data by subgroup on state assessments only
Want	Quality of implementation?	Which strategies, and why chosen?	What are student preferences for teaching?	How to recognize replicable practices early?	Impact on student achievement by subgroups?	Openings promote engagement or reduce disruption?	Early warning EOC and performance indicators (canaries)?
Learn	Gap between observed lesson plans and declared	ETS integrated, declared by teacher, observed by others	Strategies, antecedents that will engage students	Correlation between teachers and achievement	What works for all students, and what groupings close gap	Need for training, cost; anticipated student gains	Where resources and opportunities need to be created and when?
Organizational	Site-based management	Policies promoting ETS	Community aware — standards?	Need assessment calendar mandate	Relation of experience to achievement	Duplication of effort, related cost	Accountability and authority to act
Know	District policy that decisions made at sites	Policies exist, and principals to monitor ETS use	Accountability new to schools; misinformation	Lots of data never analyzed properly (all levels, sites)	Historically positive correlation, no data since 1990	Budgets tighter every year; some processes lengthy	All staff have limitations on authority to act
Want	Discretion for staff transfers, budget carryover?	Degree monitored, when, how, data?	Need for process to communicate re standards?	Correlation of achievement to testing calendars?	What is relationship between experience and achievement?	How to streamline for efficiency and effectiveness?	What artificial barriers inhibit bold, effective leadership?
Learn	Link all decisions to school goals	To disaggregate by ETS usage	Type/frequency of communication	Need for training, time, requirement	Importance of teacher longevity	Value of speed to responsiveness	How to promote creativity, risk taking

Exhibit 4.4

The Hishakawa Fishbone and Woodside Elementary School: A Cause-and-Effect Simulation

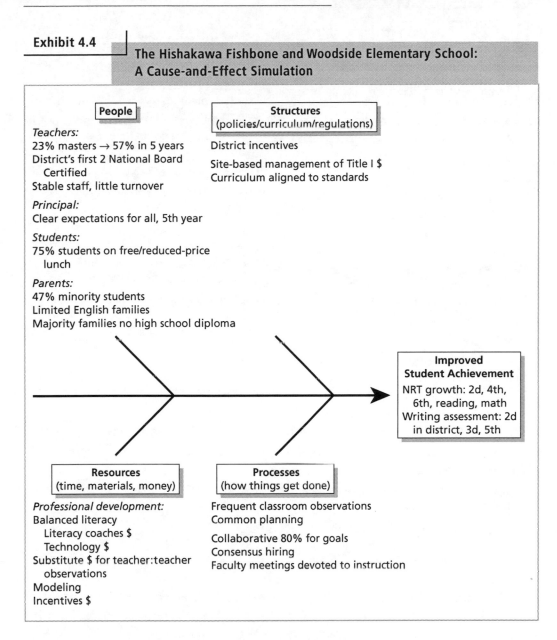

People

Teachers:
23% masters → 57% in 5 years
District's first 2 National Board
    Certified
Stable staff, little turnover

Principal:
Clear expectations for all, 5th year

Students:
75% students on free/reduced-price
    lunch

Parents:
47% minority students
Limited English families
Majority families no high school diploma

Structures
(policies/curriculum/regulations)

District incentives

Site-based management of Title I $
Curriculum aligned to standards

**Improved
Student Achievement**
NRT growth: 2d, 4th,
    6th, reading, math
Writing assessment: 2d
    in district, 3d, 5th

Resources
(time, materials, money)

Professional development:
Balanced literacy
    Literacy coaches $
    Technology $
Substitute $ for teacher:teacher
    observations
Modeling
Incentives $

Processes
(how things get done)

Frequent classroom observations
Common planning

Collaborative 80% for goals
Consensus hiring
Faculty meetings devoted to instruction

Our next tool is *force-field analysis,* a very useful tool for identifying the best available solution to persistent challenges. Begin with a goal or problem identified through a fishbone, critical incident, or flowchart analysis tool.

The next step is to identify barriers to achieving the goal, and here it is important to make sure everyone views the task as more important to solve than to explain. Groups need to practice team thinking with candor, as discussed in the data road map in Chapter 3, and practice "no blame, no shame, and no excuses." Meeting norms and operating norms for data analysis are recommended in Exhibit 4.5.

Exhibit 4.5

Group Norms for Meetings and Data Analysis

Meeting Norms	Data Analysis Norms
▪ Be on time and work as a team	▪ Establish meeting norms and reduce them to writing
▪ Respect confidentiality at all times	
▪ Be open and honest in communication	▪ Diversity of ideas: Don't meet without them
▪ Respect the speaker and be willing to disagree agreeably	▪ Homework: Come prepared to teach
▪ Understand the other person's point of view before expressing your own	▪ Roles to elicit candor: Make sure no stone (gem) is left unturned
▪ Keep comments simple and straightforward	▪ Numbers yield hunches: Don't leave meetings without one
▪ Suspend judgment regarding suggestions for change until topic is thoroughly discussed, researched, reviewed	▪ Tools are to use. Acquire and build competency in use of analysis tools
▪ Learn and share at every meeting	▪ Publish and disseminate meeting results
▪ Maintain a sense of humor	
▪ Close with a +/Δ to continually improve meeting effectiveness	

Exhibit 4.6 shows a force-field analysis aimed at finding ways to improve student achievement. To identify a powerful solution, the school examined the fishbone cause/effect analysis for success before completing a force-field analysis for its own school, narrowing barriers to achieving its goal and overcoming a very persistent problem. Note the differences between the strategies employed by the two schools as you analyze the best solution. Could you identify one primary solution to the school's perceived dilemma?

Solution: _____

The third analysis method is *decision making,* which is really a process of juxtaposing values with alternatives to prioritize the decisions that must be made. Examine Exhibit 4.7. Our last school decided to try something new and thus is faced with three choices: (1) leave things as they are (status quo); (2) adopt the "Making Standards Work" model from the Center for Performance Assessment; or (3) seriously pursue more autonomy in staffing, budgeting, and curriculum through site-based management. The district is willing to grant schools almost total site-based control if they can present a persuasive argument in favor of it. The faculty is divided, without a critical mass of support for either option, but no one is satisfied with keeping things as they are. The leadership team created a structure to keep the faculty in the decision loop, but provide some guidance to help people make their choices. Criteria have been weighted and the faculty ranked the alternatives against each criterion. Exhibit 4.7 shows the results.

Exhibit 4.6

Force-Field Analysis

1. Select problem from systems analysis tools (fishbone, 5 Ws, flowchart, critical incident) and write narrative of problem, including context. (How long has problem existed? Have there been other attempts to eliminate, mitigate?)
2. Describe barriers in terms of forces preventing resolution of problem.
3. Describe possible ways to overcome barriers as possible solutions.
4. Select solutions that best address specific elements of the problem.

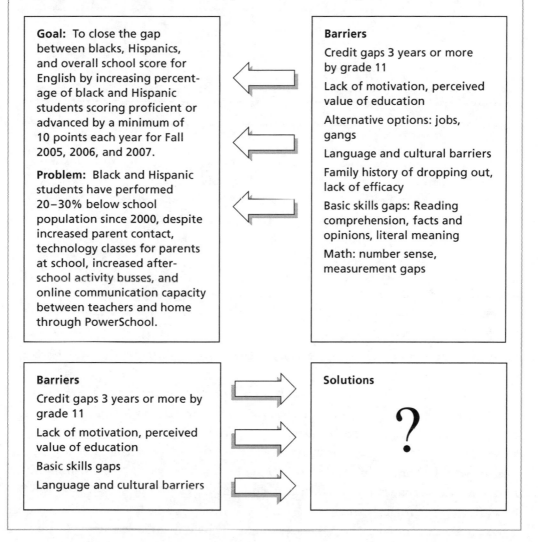

Goal: To close the gap between blacks, Hispanics, and overall school score for English by increasing percentage of black and Hispanic students scoring proficient or advanced by a minimum of 10 points each year for Fall 2005, 2006, and 2007.

Problem: Black and Hispanic students have performed 20–30% below school population since 2000, despite increased parent contact, technology classes for parents at school, increased after-school activity busses, and online communication capacity between teachers and home through PowerSchool.

Barriers

Credit gaps 3 years or more by grade 11

Lack of motivation, perceived value of education

Alternative options: jobs, gangs

Language and cultural barriers

Family history of dropping out, lack of efficacy

Basic skills gaps: Reading comprehension, facts and opinions, literal meaning

Math: number sense, measurement gaps

Barriers

Credit gaps 3 years or more by grade 11

Lack of motivation, perceived value of education

Basic skills gaps

Language and cultural barriers

Solutions

?

The leadership team identified five criteria as the major concerns the school would face, especially since the school was on adequate yearly progress (AYP) improvement. The criteria weighted a factor of five was risk to students. Respondents selected the alternative that had the least risk to student achievement. The second highest value was given

Exhibit 4.7				
Decisionmaking Model				

Alternatives	Scores 1 = low 3 = mid 5 = high			
Criteria	Weighting	Status Quo	Making Standards Work	Site-Based Management
Risk to students	5	15	25	5
NCLB pressures	4	4	20	12
Change factors	3	15	3	9
Staffing	2	6	2	10
Evidence	1	3	5	1
Totals		43	55	37

to NCLB, because of the importance of achieving and maintaining AYP. In these first two areas, faculty scored "Making Standards Work" first because of its track record of improving student achievement. Change factors addressed the pressures of new approaches and having to leave one's comfort zone, so the faculty voted for the alternative that was least apt to cause disruption and friction. Staffing was a concern, in that teachers could be reassigned involuntarily or expected to change their practices altogether; evidence, though important, was seen as integrated into other weightings.

This template has numerous applications. This scenario was created to illustrate how carefully crafted criteria, weighted with a sound rationale, can assist teams to make a decision, establish priorities, and get to work. Appendix M is the decisionmaking template.

The fourth analysis method is *clarification.* Its primary purpose is to support new practices or address controversial practices that may threaten long-standing but counterproductive traditions. The template used is simply an adaptation of note-taking strategies employed very successfully by Nan Woodson in her work with Kings Canyon School District near Fresno, California, and is one of several forms of Cornell notes. The process provides a hands-on tool with common language and process to tackle even the most difficult challenges. Exhibit 4.8 describes a situation in which leaders were expected to monitor variation in teaching practices, student achievement, and work habits with a control chart (tool to be introduced later), but the innovation is met with some resistance and a fair amount of confusion. The clarification analysis template is found in Appendix N.

The fifth method of data analysis is *action research,* a process that translates hunches from data patterns and trends into hypotheses and replicable practices. Action research

Exhibit 4.8

Clarification Analysis

Area requiring clarification:
Use of control chart and need to reduce variability

Essence of issue: (Q.)
How do I translate the need for consistency to my faculty, which prides itself on creativity and autonomy?

Known or agreed upon:	Areas of confusion/contradictions:
Variability in instructional strategies opens rather than closes the learning gap	1. What about site-based management? I need flexibility and autonomy to maximize effectiveness of my staff. 2. We differentiate instruction because of differences in teacher knowledge, skills, training, and experience, but we insist on common assessments, common instructional calendars, and common professional development. Why?

Resolution:

1. Build on the known and agreed upon; design a persuasive communication plan regarding variability in instructional practices and impact on students and a persuasive argument that consistency and creativity are not mutually exclusive

2. Recommend a rubric that articulates the craft of teaching for self-monitoring (e.g., "Framework for Teaching")

3. Recommend a second self-assessment that measures stages of concern (like concerns-based adoption model [CBAM]) for mentor teachers and induction process

4. Work with central office to design and implement a differentiated professional development model in our district

is simply a proactive hunt for a better way. After analyzing data for patterns, teachers throughout the United States of America develop hunches about relationships between instructional strategies, antecedent conditions such as materials or programs, and student achievement. Sadly, many (if not most) of these hunches become either hearsay or folklore, or are lost altogether to the profession simply because we fail to do anything about them.

Witness the story of Flora Flagg, the Milwaukee principal who introduced the notion of gathering writing samples from each teacher and scoring them herself weekly. She thereby single-handedly gave the profession a simple and effective tool to engage students in thinking and reasoning every day, in every classroom, and her school became a 90/90/90 school. Had this pioneer failed to engage in a form of action research, with assistance from the Center for Performance Assessment, only hundreds of students would have benefited rather than millions. Action research has six self-explanatory steps: (1) observe, (2) hypothesize, (3) predict, (4) test the hypothesis, (5) gather data, and (6) explain (draw inferences, conclusions, applications). Here are five suggestions for using action research:

1. Use when patterns emerging from the data suggest that something new is happening that should be verified, clarified, or discovered.

2. Study relationships between one independent variable and one dependent variable. Each reader is already very familiar with them: independent variables are the presumed causes, and dependent variables are the presumed effects. Every time you use the Hishakawa Fishbone as an analytical tool, you identify several possible action research studies.

3. Give yourself three additional ways to get started by using (a) pre/post measures on the dependent variable (dependent because we believe something depends on the cause variable), (b) correlations between the dependent variable and the presence of an isolated independent variable, and (c) comparisons with a control group (such as classrooms that are not introducing the cause variable in any systematic way).

4. For the ambitious, use simple collection tools, especially the 2×2 matrix and scattergram, to reveal three basic constructs behind statistical analysis: (a) measure of central tendency (examination of means, modes, medians), (b) measure of relationship, and (b) analysis of differences (including analysis of variance).

5. Focus on improved student achievement with your action research by beginning with proven antecedents of excellence (listed in Exhibit 4.2).

The sixth method of data analysis is *continuous improvement,* the process of improving daily routines and habits of work. Educators employ the continuous improvement form of analysis each time they rely on cycles to examine current practices and make adjustments. A very helpful tool for this method is the control chart referenced in the clarification analysis. Exhibit 4.9 shows an example of the control chart to improve routines and work habits.

Control charts give monitors of performance an early warning, the educational equivalent of the "canary in the coal mine." The standard for all five elementary schools is 60 to 80 percent of teachers using a standards-based performance assessment each term. The data clearly and quickly identifies two schools that fell below the control chart limits; if detected in the first term, the data could serve as an early-warning indicator for the two schools that are below the control limit. However, the data tells us even more. It allows those struggling to meet standards to quickly identify those to whom they may want to go for assistance. The notion of zero tolerance is a function of control charts; for issues of safety and other routines involving legal issues, control

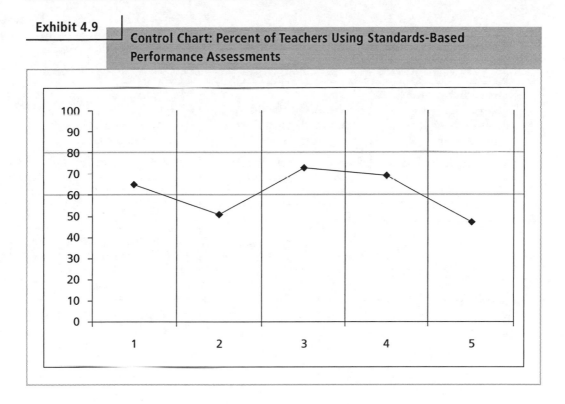

Exhibit 4.9

Control Chart: Percent of Teachers Using Standards-Based Performance Assessments

charts serve as excellent analysis tools, when there is no room for error of any kind. A control chart template is included in Appendix S.

Habits of work (work habits) include routines, procedures, and processes. Such habits of work are the only means for real improvements to occur, because someone does something differently. In terms of student achievement, the only real improvement that matters will occur at the classroom level, where teachers modify their practices and engage students in modifying their practices as well. If we are to change anything about student achievement, it must happen in our daily work habits. We must be able to examine systematically what we do with our time and how our efforts are expended.

If we learn to identify problems in our work habits, and then are able to modify and adjust them, student achievement will improve. Exhibit 4.10 offers a simple template to identify work habits and keep the focus on student achievement. Strategies, transitions, and lesson protocols all warrant some reflection to identify potential improvements in how we engage students and organize our work.

Exhibit 4.1 described each analysis method in terms of types of school data that lend themselves to that analysis. In addition, a detailed description of antecedents, collaborative activities, and accountability structures are provided to assist practitioners with their applications. Exhibit 4.11 depicts that relationship with a Venn diagram. The ease and availability of Venn diagrams make them a very useful graphic organizer

Exhibit 4.10

Process: Habits, Procedures, Routines, and Algorithms for Adult Behavior at School

Processes that contribute to improved student achievement (antecedents)?	Processes that do not contribute to improved achievement?	Processes that I am unsure about?
Written self-assessments of performance	Worksheets that address knowledge rather than analysis	Value of homework?

Exhibit 4.11

Relationship between Methods and Foundation Elements of Data Analysis

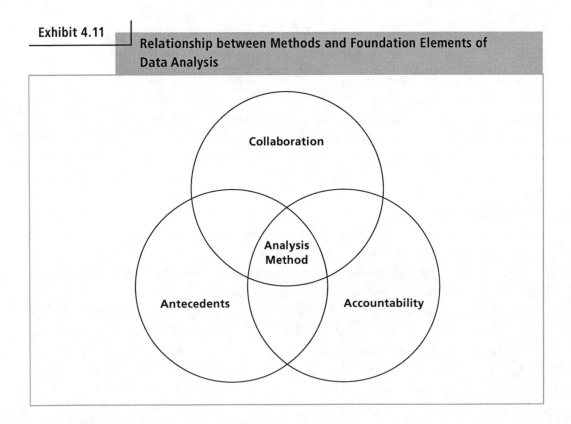

for each method of data analysis. They are particularly helpful when it is necessary to consolidate or combine existing structures. Venns are created by considering the following questions:

- What do I know about this situation?
- What are the three most important elements of this situation?
- What characteristics do the elements have in common?
- What characteristics do the elements not have in common?

SUMMARY

Several tools introduced in this chapter have wide application for discovery, research, solutions, clarification, or decisions, such as the Hishakawa Fishbone, control chart, and force-field analysis. Distinct methods have been provided to target complex challenges with precision. Some tools, such as the Hishakawa Fishbone, are robust enough to be helpful regardless of the analysis method used; others, such as action research, require a prescribed protocol to develop a preponderance of evidence and proof for the skeptic. A scoring guide for each analysis method is included in Appendix G.

DISCUSSION

BIG IDEA

Data without analysis is like standards without expectations.

QUESTIONS

1. What analysis method will be most useful to you in your current setting? Why?

Triangulation

Not everything that can be counted counts,
and not everything that counts can be counted.
— ALBERT EINSTEIN (1879–1955)

This chapter introduces the reader to *triangulation,* an approach that draws extensively on various data analysis tools but ultimately relies on the judgment of professionals to make their best decision given limited data. Triangulation is critical to using data to make visible the invisible and it is necessary if educators are to benefit fully from the methods and tools of data analysis discussed in this book. What, then, is triangulation? What is needed to effectively apply it?

TRIANGULATION TO VERIFY

Triangulation is well known to architects, engineers, and surveyors as a simple tool, widely used for centuries. To the architect, *triangulation* means discerning with precision key load factors and points in space and time from other reliable and predictable data; to the engineer and surveyor, *triangulation* means calibrating unknown points with precision in space and time on the basis of existing data and irregularly distributed samples of data. For both professions, triangulation uses a variety of forms of existing data to find a desired and unknown reference point. When the surveyor needs to estimate the height of a point on the land surface, she utilizes samples of soil composition, density variation, contours, weather patterns, and a host of other data. A sextant (a triangulation tool used by mariners) allowed explorers to plot the globe by triangulating the stars with each other and the horizon to ascertain longitude and latitude at sea.

Thus, triangulation is a means of determining precise targets with limited information. Exhibit 5.1 provides examples of achievement data triangulated by antecedent, collaboration, and accountability structures to reveal relative influences on student performance. If their teachers systematically identified antecedents, collaborated around student work, or maintained specific accountability structures, those scoring proficient or advanced are indicated by the symbol ✪ placed in all affected circles. Thirty-three of the hundred students in equal enrollment classes were proficient on the math assessment. Reflect on the lessons from this visual triangulation.

Exhibit 5.1

Triangulation of Math Assessments

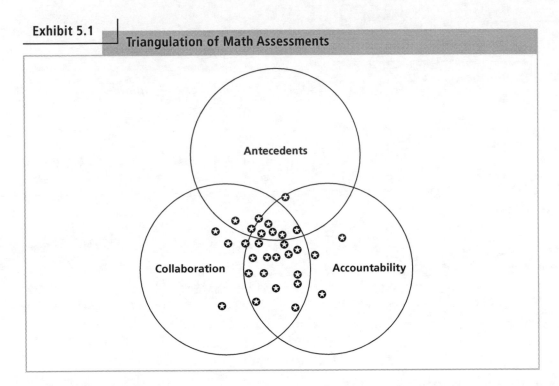

Exhibit 5.2

Triangulation of Data by Teams

	Team A	Team B	Team C	Teacher D
Proficient math assessment	60%	20%	40%	15%
Data team meetings/semester	4	1	3	1
Expository writing required daily	Yes	No	Yes	No
EOCs developed collaboratively	Yes	No	No	No
Assessment calendars applied to assessments	80%	No	No	No
Teachers with authority to be accountable	Yes	No	No	No

In Exhibit 5.2, the same data is presented across four teams at the school, offering a different slice of the triangulation data. Complete the exercise by recording one insight you observe and one recommendation for the future.

Observation from Exhibits 5.1 and 5.2? _____

_____

_____

Recommendation? _____

_____

_____

    A number of conclusions can be drawn from this example to improve performance of teams B, C, and D especially, even though data seldom provides such direct and powerful correlations. The chi-square test, a nonparametric test of significance, could tell us there were significant differences due to the departure from expected proportions in certain cells, but the triangulation you just completed helped identify practices that work and those that do not. A valuable aspect of triangulation is the way it sets the stage for each of us to check our assumptions at the door when it comes to data analysis.

IT'S NOT ABOUT PERFECTION

One problem with data analysis in schools today is the fact that the data available is never perfect and seldom even complete at any one point in time. The triangulation process has been employed for centuries for the very purpose of gleaning meaning from imperfect and incomplete data. The complexity of education compels us to look for patterns and trends, in a practical sense, that lead us to decisions that improve student achievement. When data is triangulated, each point serves as a check on the other dimension, with the desired outcome the realization of new insights from the various data points (and types) that are not available from examining only one type of data (e.g., achievement) or one perspective. Tools like the wagon wheel and the triangulation template allow you to mix and match any data your teams deem important. Use the triangulation template to determine what should be done to raise third-grade math assessments. Exhibit 5.3 shows the results, and yes, I know they are limited.

THE WAGON WHEEL

Exhibit 5.4 introduces a data analysis tool that enables teachers and principals to conduct multivariate analyses without having to be expert in statistical analysis. There are ten concentric circles in Exhibit 5.4, simply because it lends itself to metric scales of ten, such as percent. The beauty of the wagon wheel/spider chart is that one can use different scales for each spoke and still retain integrity of the analysis. To illustrate the

Exhibit 5.3

Triangulation Exercise: Third-Grade Mathematics

You've just received notice that you will be allowed to make any changes necessary to raise third-grade math scores with existing resources. Budgets are tight, but you can move positions, change schedules, abandon curriculum, and redirect materials budgets as you see fit. The problem is that you have to decide your course of action sometime before you finish reading this book, and no additional data is available.

Ground Rules

1. You must triangulate data by examining antecedents, collaboration, and the degree to which accountability is operating. Remember, accountability has three components:
   - Responsibility for results
   - Authority to commit and redirect resources
   - Permission to subtract obsolete, wasteful, and inefficient practices.

2. You must complete the triangulation using the KWL framework:
   - What do we **Know** from these data? (patterns, trends, similarities, differences, outliers)
   - What do we **Want** to find out? (decide on purpose of analysis)
   - What do we need to **Learn**, and how will we know we learned it? (choose a preferred analysis method)

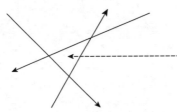

Triangulation
is the key to
accurate location.

Related Data for Third-Grade Math

Achievement Data/Curriculum	Collaboration Data	Antecedent Data	Accountability Evidence
+Gap closed for Hispanic only ☺	+All teachers collaboratively score writing weekly ☺	+Problem of the Week: All classrooms ☺	−Board homework policy mandates 20 math problems nightly ☹
−Cohort scores, no gain/3 years ☹	−Common planning time is used for individual lesson planning ☹	−No performance assessments aligned to math standard ☹	+Teachers trained in performance assessments, free to write assessments ☺
+Number sense highest area, all subgroups ☺	−Teachers construct math assessments for classrooms ☹	−Math standards not posted any class ☹	+Teachers not bound by textbook, free to supplement ☺

(continues)

Exhibit 5.3

Triangulation Exercise: Third-Grade Mathematics *(Continued)*

Related Data for Third-Grade Math *(Continued)*

Achievement Data/Curriculum	Collaboration Data	Antecedent Data	Accountability Evidence
− Problem solving is lowest area, all subgroups but Asian students ☹	− Teachers follow district curriculum calendar, not state standards ☹	− One teacher uses power standards, others use text ☹	− Math time diminished in favor of literacy by principal's directive ☹
− Math never integrated with other content ☹	+ State department Web site has exemplar lesson plans in math ☺	− All teachers use worksheets daily for homework ☹	Full-time math coach works with students in pullout ?
− Instructional calendars emphasize number sense ☹	+ District summer school opportunities include two weeks of training with pay if teams attend ☺	− All teachers return papers with letter grades only, no specific corrective feedback ☹	− Teacher evaluation is binomial checklist: Met Standard or Doesn't Meet only options; 27 items ☹
+ In-service last year on "Five Easy Steps" (2 days) ☺	− Substitute shortage eliminated observation of colleagues ☹	+ Class size for all three classes is less than 20 students ☺	+ Annual goals must align with standards ☺

Discuss with colleagues what new *learning, insights, awareness,* and *recommendations* can be surmised from triangulating this data exercise:

1. _____

_____

_____

2. _____

_____

_____

3. _____

_____

_____

Exhibit 5.3

Triangulation Exercise: Third-Grade Mathematics *(Continued)*

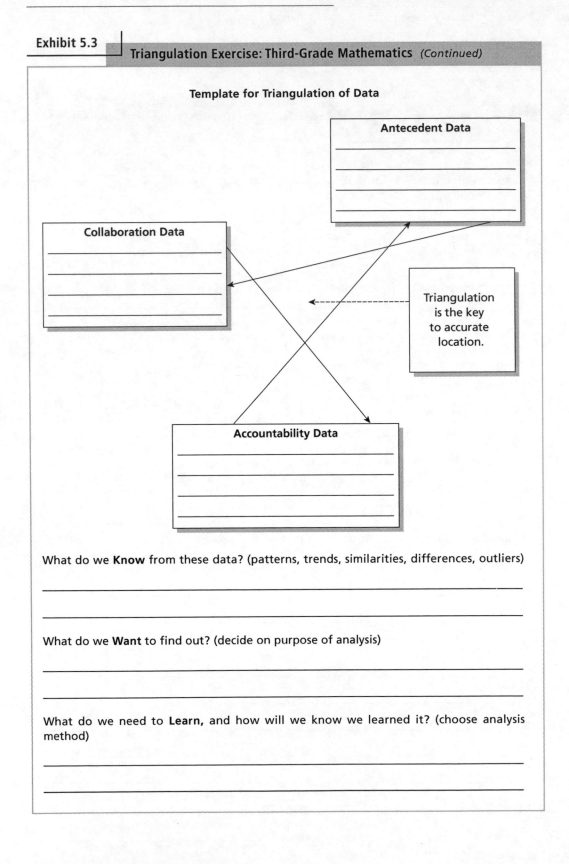

Template for Triangulation of Data

Antecedent Data

Collaboration Data

Triangulation
is the key
to accurate
location.

Accountability Data

What do we **Know** from these data? (patterns, trends, similarities, differences, outliers)

What do we **Want** to find out? (decide on purpose of analysis)

What do we need to **Learn,** and how will we know we learned it? (choose analysis method)

Exhibit 5.4

The Wagon-Wheel Data Analysis Tool and Graphic Organizer

Steps in Using Wagon Wheels

1. Assign key variables to each spoke on wheel (10).

2. Collect data across key variables.

3. Establish scale for each spoke, with highest performance on outer rim of circle. Label each individual spoke with its own scale.

4. Plot performance data along spokes, color-coding to distinguish units being compared (classrooms, schools, departments, grade levels, budgets, even certification areas).

5. Connect lines for each unit if comparisons are made between units.

6. Identify the pattern of performance against selected performance standards.

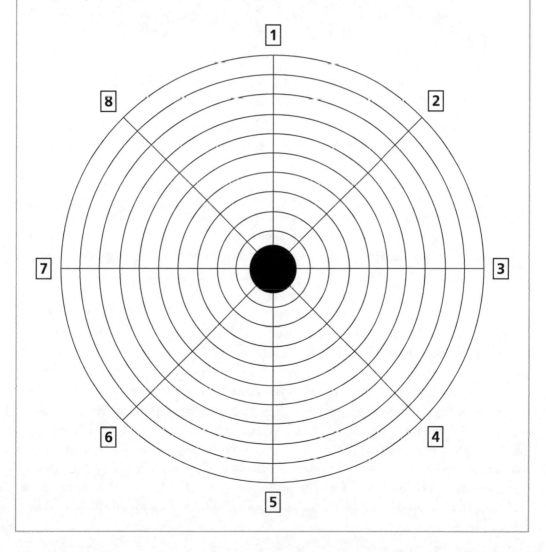

robust capacity of this simple tool, the following diverse variables have been selected for wagon-wheel spokes in our first example:

1. Budget projections. Budgeted-to-actual expenditures reveal degree of precision and accuracy for administrators with 100 percent standard for excellence.

2. Use of technology. Degree of variability within entities in terms of fluency and application of end-user technologies, such as software applications. Measurement will be percentage used proficiently, based on seven Microsoft Office Suite applications (i.e., Microsoft Word, Excel, Publisher, etc.).

3. Percent of total student assessments subject to assessment calendars at school.

4. Reduction of classroom interruptions (e.g., intercom announcements/day) measured in raw numbers (range 0–10).

5. Classroom checklist for standards implementation (see Exhibit 3.5), measured in terms of percent of fourteen items monitored by teacher.

6. Percent proficient on the state writing assessment.

7. Teacher absence rates, measured by average number of days out of classroom per teacher for any reason for the last twelve-month period.

8. Time lag between special education referral and delivery of specialized instructional services, measured by total referrals/school days between referral and first day of service (range 1–100).

Exhibit 5.5 illustrates the visual power of the wagon wheel to reveal discrepancies, strengths, and weaknesses. For the purpose of simplicity, three classrooms have been selected as units of comparison, even though spokes 1, 7, and perhaps 8 are administrative indicators that are unlikely to be selected as variables by teachers. The other variables, however, provide both administrators and teachers with valuable information that can help in setting priorities, identifying antecedents, and initiating improvements.

The data reveals areas of strength and weakness for all three classrooms. Classroom C performed much closer to standard on all instructional areas, while classroom B was furthest away from the desired performance on all but teacher absences, with the lowest percent proficient on the state writing assessment. Classroom B lagged in technology literacy and needs immediate assistance to reach the desired levels.

A second application that illustrates the versatility of this tool is an examination of teacher performance or leadership performance based on a rubric (Danielson, 1996; Reeves, 2004c). For this application, the spokes would represent a self-assessment, a peer assessment, and a supervisor assessment for a single teacher or principal. Think about the usefulness of that process, whereby professionals could refine and calibrate understanding about their own performance. Appendix P provides a template for the wagon-wheel data analysis tool.

Exhibit 5.5

Wagon Wheel for Classrooms A, B, and C

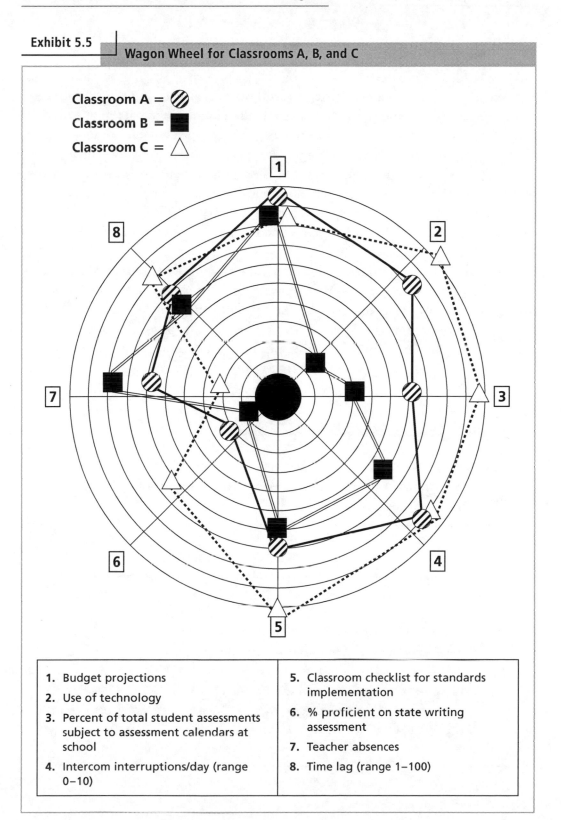

1. Budget projections
2. Use of technology
3. Percent of total student assessments subject to assessment calendars at school
4. Intercom interruptions/day (range 0–10)
5. Classroom checklist for standards implementation
6. % proficient on state writing assessment
7. Teacher absences
8. Time lag (range 1–100)

SUMMARY

Triangulation is a process of discovering the unknown by looking at things from different angles. It necessitates diversity of ideas, experiences, and perspectives, and therefore requires a healthy dose of collaboration. It also requires solid data points to triangulate from, whether the data describes results in student achievement, compliance with policies and procedures, or monitoring of the quality and degree with which proven instructional strategies are deployed. It therefore requires a healthy dose of accountability as well, empowering people to take responsibility not only for their actions, but also for results. Accountability requires authority to take action on the basis of data and permission to clean house and sweep away obsolete and counterproductive practices and programs when needed.

Triangulation reveals understanding that data standing alone cannot, as we discovered in the wagon-wheel exercise. As educators, we must be prepared to respond to such discoveries; this is a moral imperative to make a difference for the students we serve. That requires leadership and accountability, and the capacity to create a sense of urgency when the data indicates a need for decisive and courageous actions. Appendix G contains a detailed rubric describing proficiency in utilizing triangulation.

DISCUSSION

Big Idea

Triangulation is a process of discovering the unknown by looking at things from different angles.

Questions

1. *What is the relationship between triangulation and accountability in data analysis? Collaboration?*

2. *What is the benefit of developing triangulations to examine effects data, antecedent data, and measures of accountability?*

3. *Consider designing your own wagon wheel with another colleague who is familiar with your school or position. Collaborate to identify the variables that are most important to your work.*

Replication

Get the habit of analysis—analysis will in time enable synthesis to become your habit of mind.

— FRANK LLOYD WRIGHT (1869–1959)

Teachers and teaching are treasure chests of innovation and inspiration, and we need a means to capture, expand, and apply those practices that work best to as many settings as possible, to reach as many students as possible. Replication of good ideas should be the reason we analyze data in the first place—to extend what works as quickly and efficiently as possible. Replication and subtraction are nothing less than the evidence of a dynamic and effective data management system. If schools fail to replicate best practices or to eliminate unsound, ineffective practices, where is the improvement?

Data analysis is the parent of action research and replication. This chapter attempts to ensure that replication of best practices becomes the norm for successful practices rather than the exception it has been for so long. We begin by introducing the discrepancy chart as a means to illustrate the difficulty in waiting for achievement data to shout at us to replicate.

A discrepancy chart establishes a standard of performance and depicts performance along a horizontal line. Performances exceeding the standard are represented by bars or data points above the line and performances not yet at the desired standard are represented by data points or bars below the line. Exhibits 6.1 and 6.2 compare actual student performance against predicted performance. For this data, a value of zero means that the actual score was the same as the predicted score. A positive value means that, on average, students outperformed their demographics and academic history, and a negative value indicates the opposite.

By 2000, students in Elementary School 1 were outperforming their demographics by almost 1.7 standard deviations. Scrutinize the data for the same time period for Elementary School 2. Because both schools have very similar student body demographics, and because both schools are part of the same school system and enjoy the same

Exhibit 6.1

Hypothetical Sixth-Grade Language Mechanics: Elementary School 1

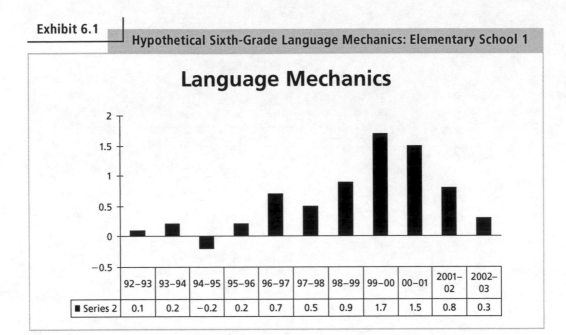

Language Mechanics

	92–93	93–94	94–95	95–96	96–97	97–98	98–99	99–00	00–01	2001–02	2002–03
■ Series 2	0.1	0.2	−0.2	0.2	0.7	0.5	0.9	1.7	1.5	0.8	0.3

Exhibit 6.2

Hypothetical Sixth-Grade Language Mechanics: Elementary School 2

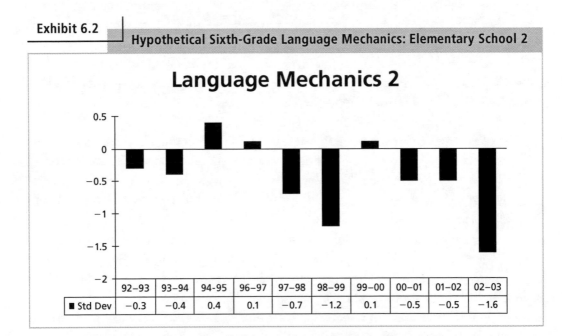

Language Mechanics 2

	92–93	93–94	94–95	96–97	97–98	98–99	99–00	00–01	01–02	02–03
■ Std Dev	−0.3	−0.4	0.4	0.1	−0.7	−1.2	0.1	−0.5	−0.5	−1.6

resources, reasonable people should agree that School 2 needs some help, whereas School 1 had ten of eleven years in which students outperformed their demographics.

The question now is: When was the most opportune time to begin looking for replicable practices? In 1994–1995, School 2 looked like the successful school, at least in terms of gains in Language Mechanics. In 1995–1996, differences were negligible;

1997–1998 was the first year School 2 scores showed a serious decline. If teams waited until the millennium to look for patterns, they would have found that both schools had begun to decline from previous years' scores. It would have been easy to explain away the small, incremental differences between these schools, and to miss the opportunity to learn from the distinctions that warrant a second look. In contrast, after waiting several years, attuned professionals attentive to the data might have called for a closer look, and found those antecedents at School 1 that could help School 2. We need to ask ourselves, in this era of standards and accountability, whether we have several years to wait. We need to find ways for practices that are true antecedents of excellence to be replicated in earnest, take stock of lessons learned, and make adjustments to improve student achievement. We need a recipe for replication.

RECIPE FOR REPLICATION

Recipes are ideas that are rapidly disseminated, are replicated easily and with little oversight, and can be implemented with sustainable quality. Recipes are replicated because participants are able to experience their benefits firsthand and there is immediate feedback, measured against a standard that the chef adjusts to. They are simply step-by-step innovations that are reproduced and multiplied with precision and care. Thus, recipes serve as a useful analogy for replicating best practices. Exhibit 6.3 identifies a number of strategies to facilitate making replication as common and pervasive as copying and replicating recipes.

QUICK, GET THE CAMERA!

Stephen Covey (1996) describes a "third person learning" process to share knowledge and skills by teaching someone what you have just learned. He offers three basic steps that apply to our discussion of replication: capture, expand, and apply. Just as we use digital cameras to capture the moment, we need to develop a work habit to capture evidence of success—even incremental, qualitative evidence like a smile or a raised hand or on-time attendance for the high school junior who lets everyone in class know every day that she doesn't like being there. All of these can be objectively measured and monitored and provide meaningful Tier 3 data about student performance. Such data contributes to a robust capacity to recognize replicable practices early, rather than waiting for changes in achievement data only (as our example showed with Schools 1 and 2).

The camera analogy goes further than this snapshot application, however. Digital cameras are first and foremost easy to use—so easy that major film companies are abandoning film photographs completely in recognition that the future is digital. Data must be user-friendly to reduce its costs. "Catch them doing something good" is a great strategy. Recording the good they were doing is even better.

Exhibit 6.3

Strategies to Promote Replication

	External (between schools, across districts)	Internal (within schools, departments, grades)
School and District	■ Disseminate results of data team minutes to like colleagues at other schools via Web sites, email; omit student names and other confidential data ■ Quarterly, disseminate/present to other schools data charts/graphs of ideas borrowed, ideas given away, and results ■ Develop a Q&A communiqué that invites ideas, strategies, and structures to address real student and teacher needs in real time; rotate responsibility for developing answers from school to school ■ Establish an electronic "We Made a Difference" data wall ■ Define a preponderance of evidence that will suffice to initiate external, school-to-school or district-wide replication	■ Establish a "We Made a Difference" data wall (electronic or physical) that monitors the number and type of interventions that have been implemented, with accompanying results ■ Principal establishes expectation of receiving weekly reports of "ideas I borrowed," "ideas I gave away," and results from ideas ■ Add a column to the "We Made a Difference" data wall labeled "Learning Opportunities," where results were less than immediate ■ Create standing agenda items for meetings: What works well for whom, why, and how do you know? ■ Define a preponderance of evidence that will suffice to initiate internal replication
Classroom	■ Identify students whose behavior or performance have turned around; verify with data ■ Value observation data as much as numbers data ■ Disseminate classroom practices that save time (Q&A or "We Made a Difference" data walls) ■ Disseminate classroom practices that students would like repeated (Q&A or "We Made a Difference" data walls) ■ Disseminate classroom practices that increased collaboration (Q&A or "We Made a Difference" data walls)	■ Create and institutionalize "What's Working" meetings with recorders and group responsibility (verify preponderance of evidence, what works well for whom, and why) ■ All teachers submit to principal a list of "ideas I borrowed" and "ideas I gave away" each week ■ Early replication signals: evidence of changes, enthusiasm, indicators, students outperforming their demographics ■ Identify classroom practices that: □ Save time □ Students would like repeated □ Increase collaboration

ACTION RESEARCH

Action research was introduced in Chapter 4 as an analysis method, but it is also a vehicle for replication, although it involves a more formal process than either third-person learning or recipe replication. In 1994, Emily Calhoun recommended three levels of action research that continue to work for action and replication:

1. Teacher as individual researcher
2. Collaborative action research
3. School-wide action research

Action research as described in Exhibit 6.4 has six self-explanatory steps.

Exhibit 6.4

Steps of Action Research

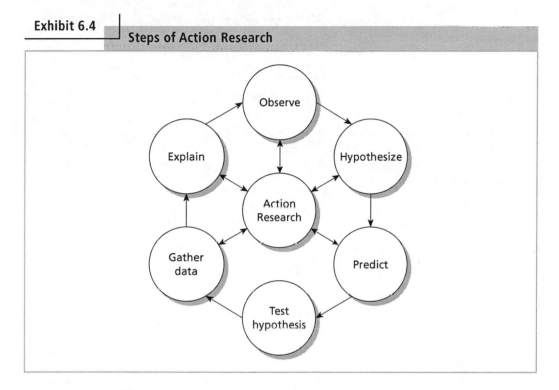

Action research is the kind of analysis warranted when there is a desire to replicate externally. It is the process of verifying results achieved using the same problems and variables, but with variations in terms of who, when, and where. A general rule of thumb for action research is:

Use action research when patterns emerging from the data suggest that something new is happening that should be verified, clarified, or discovered.

PERMISSION TO SUBTRACT

In Chapter 1, *accountability* was defined as including not only responsibility for results, but also the authority to act (commit resources) and permission to subtract. Without the latter, replication will be stymied as well. All of us can remember instances when an innovative and important idea was shelved simply because an existing program interfered with its introduction. Exhibit 6.5 delineates questions to help determine whether and when to subtract obsolete or ineffective practices.

Exhibit 6.5

Subtracting Obsolete or Ineffective Practices

Subtraction

	Yes	No
1. Does the practice/resource yield data about teaching or learning?	❏	❏
2. Does the practice/resource address specific content standards?	❏	❏
3. Does the practice/resource provide diagnostic data about student achievement?	❏	❏
4. Does the practice invite collaboration with colleagues?	❏	❏
5. Is there data supporting the need for or value of the practice/ resource to improve student achievement in my classroom?	❏	❏
6. Is there a corresponding or competing practice/resource that accomplishes the same end/result?	❏	❏

Yes to three or fewer questions: The practice or resource should be subtracted in some measure.

Yes to four or more questions: The practice or resource should be retained or possibly replicated.

Replacement

	Yes	No
7. Can the same practice/resource be accomplished through other means, such as improved technology?	❏	❏
8. Can the practice/resource be omitted and still achieve the same result?	❏	❏
9. Can the same result be accomplished in less instructional time?	❏	❏
10. Can the same result be accomplished in less preparation time?	❏	❏
11. Can the same result be accomplished with less expense in time, talent, and resources?	❏	❏

Yes to three or fewer questions: The practice or resource should be replaced at a prescribed time.

Yes to four or more questions: The practice or resource should be replaced as soon as possible.

SUMMARY

Replication is probably the best indicator of a high-quality, effective system of data analysis. It represents efforts by educators to multiply what works, and epitomizes continuous improvement. It is intensely personal, and will seldom occur in earnest at the classroom level if teachers do not experience the benefit of adopting the practice firsthand. Replication has traditionally been associated with large-scale change efforts, programmatic changes, and even professional development models. It should become much more pervasive and much more automatic if we are to build the capacity we need to respond to student needs.

This chapter provided several suggestions for facilitating a functional and dynamic system for replication. "What's working?" meetings and "We Made a Difference" data walls can go a long way to facilitate those work habits that result in the everyday replication that is as common as sharing a favorite recipe. Appendix G contains a comprehensive scoring guide for replicating best practices in data analysis.

DISCUSSION

BIG IDEA

Replication is simply making sure that what works very well for a few students is available to as many students as possible.

QUESTIONS

1. *Are there early indicators for replication in your current position? What could be done to make sure they are operating?*

2. *What kinds of things should be defined to establish a foundation for replication?*

CHAPTER 7

Data and Leadership

*Accountability for quality belongs to
top management. It cannot be delegated.*
— W. Edwards Deming (1900–1993)

W. Edwards Deming was the most highly respected expert on quality in the twentieth century. His point was not about the omnipotence of leaders in positions of authority—quite the contrary. When a teacher sets expectations for a paper and students produce less than what is expected, the teacher, as a leader, has a choice. She can say, "Oh well, you tried. Here's your grade." Or the teacher can provide corrective feedback from beginning to completion, adjusting instruction to challenge every learner, utilizing effective scoring guides to scaffold the journey, and at every step, teaching and clarifying the standard of quality. *Assessing Educational Leaders* (Reeves, 2004c) outlines a standards-based approach to leadership assessment that crafts ten dimensions into a performance matrix, with explicit descriptors of proficiency and a laser-like focus on reciprocal and corrective feedback. The tools and structures described in *Show Me the Proof!* require that level of leadership to translate the lessons of the data into action.

Leadership is always about action—proactive action taken on the basis of informed, reflective, and collaborative analysis. The following acts of leadership are needed to apply the tools, strategies, and structures described thus far. Leadership:

- Establishes organizational values
- Aligns efforts around a clear and common purpose
- Promotes innovation
- Reviews performance
- Communicates expectations, directions, and values

These actions of leadership will guide the discussion of the next four additions to your toolkit. Each tool requires the resilience of leadership to maintain a relentless focus on achievement, challenge colleagues for their best thinking, and insist that action follow analysis.

SIDE-BY-SIDE ANALYSIS

Our first tool is the principal's leadership opportunity, the side-by-side analysis, depicted in Exhibit 7.1. *Side-by-side analysis* is the process of aligning state standards with the curriculum, state assessments, and all local assessments. The format examines data from the classroom, course, or grade population from subgroups to individual students. It reviews performance and aligns efforts to ensure that curriculum, instructional responses, and resources are focused appropriately. Leaders who expect teachers to complete side-by-side analyses communicate the value and expectation that each teacher will become an expert about his or her students, standards, and assessments, and aligns efforts around a clear and common purpose.

Acts of leadership. If data indicates poor alignment between standards and curriculum, but some students do very well on the state assessment, the team would have good reason to apply a fishbone or critical incident or flowchart to determine what factors (antecedents) led to such stellar results. If the curriculum was aligned very well with both standards and state assessment, but certain subgroups performed very poorly on the assessment, a team may be inclined to use a relations diagram, Venn diagram, or force-field analysis to identify the barriers inhibiting improved performance and develop solutions that could make a difference. The value of the side-by-side analysis will be contingent on whether efforts to triangulate data address collaborative opportunities, accountability structures, and antecedents of excellence from the research, best practices, and local evidence.

LISTENING SYSTEMS

This section examines the ability of a multifaceted listening system to systematically gather feedback from stakeholders. Virtually all schools and districts conduct satisfaction surveys with parents; they do so less often with staff, and rarely with students. The results are typically addressed in a single school improvement goal, reviewed annually after the administration of a predetermined yearly parent survey. In this era of accountability, high stakes, and evidence of high reward in terms of student achievement when schools put all the pieces together, it behooves us to go beyond a listening system that is limited to satisfaction. Exhibit 7.2 shows a completed listening system that examines the level of implementation across three dimensions, with recommendations.

Referring once more to the acts of leadership, the reader will note that the framework does in fact examine the degree to which efforts are aligned around a common purpose. It critically challenges schools to take advantage of listening data to promote

Exhibit 7.1 Side-by-Side Analysis of Curriculum, Assessments, Standards, and Data Tools

	Test Performance	Common Assessment Performance	Standards Addressed	Curriculum: Level/Grade/Course/Unit	Analysis Tool(s)
Population					
Subgroup					
Student					
Population					
Subgroup					
Student					
Population					
Subgroup					
Student					
Population					
Subgroup					
Student					

Findings from triangulation (patterns, gaps) _____

Conclusion and decision _____

Key to Analysis Tools Abbreviations:

Celeration chart	Cel	Flowchart	F	Relations diagram	R
Control chart	Con	Force-field analysis	FF	Triangulation	T
Critical incident	CI	Hishakawa Fishbone	C/E	Venn diagram	V
Discrepancy chart	D	Plus/Delta	Δ	Wagon-wheel chart	WW

87

Exhibit 7.2 | Sample Listening Data (Milford School District)

School: _____ Principal: _____ Date: _____ Email: _____

Satisfaction Surveys	Parents	Teachers and Administrators	Staff	Students	Patrons	P	I	E	Rationale: Current Practice
What do we currently do with the data?	Look at it; address top-concern area as one SIP goal	Gather; tabulate, publish, discuss with faculty; address in SIP	Gather; tabulate; publish report to all staff	Student council coordinates survey; published in school newspaper	Surveys limited to bond issue and mill levy campaigns; election team review			✔	Satisfaction surveys have been in place for 11 years. Few changes implemented as a result; survey results vary little from year to year; emphasis/ monitoring on % responding.
Authority to act? (commit resources)	Established through SIP process	Not defined	Not defined	Student council may propose recommended changes to principal through advisor	Primarily to assess level of community support; action related to campaigns	✔			Authority to act has always been assumed. Only parent and faculty satisfaction surveys result in action and even then may be limited to an activity or objective in the SIP. Very limited patron and community efforts other than Web site communications.

P = Proposed   I = Introduced   E = Established

(continues)

Exhibit 7.2

Sample Listening Data (Milford School District) *(Continued)*

School: Principal: Date: Email:

Satisfaction Surveys	Parents	Teachers and Administrators	Staff	Students	Patrons	P	I	E	Rationale: Current Practice
Who?/When?	SIP leadership team; May of each year	Principal holds key; annually in May	Principal; annually in May	Advisor coordinates, facilitates review; as needed	No other process to act on patron concerns		✔		Administrative function; some cooperation with teacher representatives; rare to collaborate or insist on action to follow. All data examined at end of year, with numerous competing priorities!
How?	Team reviews results, discusses outcomes	Presentation at faculty meeting; Q&A held to clarify and explain status quo; changes rarely made	Written report distributed	Council forwards to advisor who forwards to administration	N/A. No process exists outside of efforts to secure votes	✔			Action is generally discussion or completion of a report. Wide variability in terms of structure that connects results to action. Format for action often misses key opportunities.

Summary of Satisfaction Listening System:
Satisfaction is the most established listening format for Milford, with routine inclusion in school improvement plans for parents and teachers. Student feedback is obscured through organizational layers; little evidence exists of a predictable and viable cycle. Action taken on the basis of satisfaction data is random at best.

P = Proposed   I = Introduced   E = Established

(continues)

Exhibit 7.2

Sample Listening Data (Milford School District) (Continued)

School: Principal: Date: Email:

Focus Groups, Interviews	Parents	Teachers and Administrators	Staff	Students	Patrons	P	I	E	Rationale: Current Practice
What do we currently do with the data?	No data	Faculty meeting minutes; no process to gather open-ended data from faculty	No data	Topic-driven focus groups (e.g., dress code, open campus)	Superintendent conducts quarterly "town meetings"		✓		Few elements in place; need to make sure current data is analyzed and responded to.
Authority to act? (commit resources)	N/A	Not defined	N/A	Not defined	Superintendent has authority, limited by policy	✓			Ambiguous format for taking action; totally situational.
Who?/When?	N/A	No systematic process in place; as needed	N/A	Principal directs actions	Superintendent responds to situations	✓			Little assurance that action will follow input.
How?	N/A	Principal assesses need and responds	N/A	Direct, by delegate, or consensus	Varied responses to concerns	✓			Administrative prerogative.
Web Site	**Parents**	**Teachers and Administrators**	**Staff**	**Students**	**Patrons**	**P**	**I**	**E**	**Rationale: Current Practice**
What do we currently do with the data?	Complaint review by leadership team; acts on select complaints	Teachers and administrators have individual Web sites for communication	Discretion to create and respond to Web site	Same chance as parents to respond to school officials	Same chance as parents to respond to school officials	✓			Plan to respond to complaint/concern next year based on technology.

P = Proposed   I = Introduced   E = Established

(continues)

Exhibit 7.2 Sample Listening Data (Milford School District) (Continued)

School: Principal: Date: Email:

Web Site	Parents	Teachers and Administrators	Staff	Students	Patrons	P	I	E	Rationale: Current Practice
Authority to act? (commit resources)	Leadership team grants authority to act if complaint is viewed as having merit	All have authority to respond to concerns or suggestions within job description or sphere of influence	Staff are expected to respond to all concerns	No format for response to students	No format for response to patrons, except phone policy of 48 hours	✔			No standards in place at present; action taken varies by administrative discretion; reactive.
Who?/When?	Administrators, department chairs, counselors; no response standard	Response based on concern raised and time constraints; no response standard	Staff respond as with phone policy (48 hours)	No requirement or timeframe standard exists	No requirement or timeframe standard exists	✔			No systematic connection from process for input to action taken.
How?	Principal assigns responsibility	Collaboration; modify instruction, materials, time, and opportunity	Email, involve others	N/A	N/A	✔			Wide discretion to administrators; no standard for action.

Summary of Focus Group/Interview and Web Site Listening Systems:
Focus groups and Web site listening systems are neither systematic nor reliable; response standards are nonexistent; need for standards, processes, accountability. Systems fail to adhere to guidelines, even though capacity exists for transparency and user-friendly technology is available.

P = Proposed   I = Introduced   E = Established

innovation, and the framework communicates expectations not only that stakeholders will be listened to, but also that their input will be valued and used. A template for listening systems is found in Appendix U.

PLUS/DELTA (+/Δ)

Plus/delta is a common reflection tool designed to improve the quality of meetings. Because meetings are the primary facilitators of team thinking and the synergy that results from effective collaboration, it is important that efforts be made to make meetings as effective and meaningful as possible. A template for plus/delta is provided in Appendix V, in addition to the "Meeting Norms" template in Appendix R.

Delta (Δ) is the Greek symbol for "change in" (Downing & Clark, 1997, x). It provides a convenient way to reflect on the value of any group process or meaning and to do so in a positive, proactive manner. Its purpose is to continually improve (make change in) the quality of dialogue at meetings and to enlist the collective wisdom of participating teams to improve effectiveness as well. Actually, +/Δ is designed to stimulate reflection on what went well (emphasis on meeting results and outcomes, rather than people) and what should be improved (emphasis on the process rather than individuals). As a standards-based approach, the focus is on results and work habits that can be improved. It is all about alignment of vision and purpose with action, and is itself clear evidence of what the organization values and what directions it will set to promote those values. Six steps describe the plus/delta process.

1. Following any group activity, ask someone to serve as a recorder on one side of the room with a flipchart labeled "+."

2. Ask a second person to serve as a recorder on the other side of the room with a flipchart labeled "Δ."

3. Set the ground rules by asking the audience to identify what worked well in the meeting just concluded that warrants repetition in similar future meetings. The responses to that question are recorded on the plus chart.

4. Ask the audience to identify what aspects of the process could be improved. The suggestions for improvement are recorded on the delta chart.

5. It is important that everyone understand that this is not a process for identifying positives or negatives, and that no personal references (even positive) are part of +/Δ. Stick to what events and behaviors are worth replicating, and which events and behaviors could be improved and how.

6. Note that both plus and delta will yield helpful, instructive feedback and encourage participants to think as a team and look forward.

LOGARITHMIC CHART

The final tool tracks data more accurately for forecasting time-referenced data (e.g., budgets, enrollments, weather). Exhibit 7.3 illustrates. By looking at enrollment growth on a typical equal-interval chart, we anticipate growth using a trend line at around 40,000 additional students from year 6 to year 10. However, by applying the same trend line to a logarithmic chart, we predict enrollment growth at closer to 80,000 additional students in the same period. Is it better to know such information up front or after the fact? Apply the same rule to longitudinal trends in assessments.

Exhibit 7.3

Comparison of Forecasts Using Logarithmic versus Equal-Interval Scales

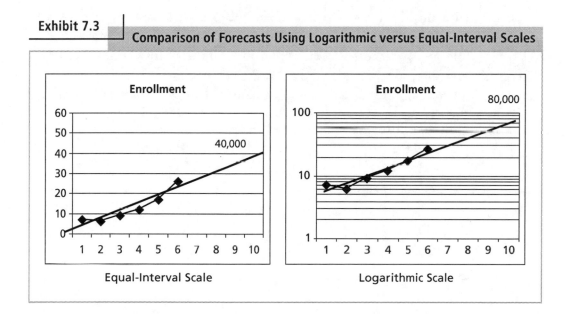

Equal-Interval Scale   Logarithmic Scale

Although our example is hypothetical, the consequences of using faulty projections are enormous; hence the use of logarithmic charts is recommended for time-referenced data, including student achievement. Academic growth will always appear greater on an equal-interval chart, as will academic declines. Downing and Clark (1997) warn that in any instance in which time is a variable, the starting point for a vertical scale should be zero. To do otherwise skews the results, showing increases and declines at a much steeper slope than reality warrants. Anticipation that a significant number of students will meet adequate yearly progress (AYP) without additional and more focused interventions can provide a false sense of confidence and result in missed opportunities.

The forecasting chart will not and cannot improve student achievement. It is just one more tool to help us realistically face the issues before us and plan with a better understanding of what it will really take to reach the ambitious goals set by our communities and ourselves. A forecasting chart template is found in Appendix W.

SUMMARY

The themes of action and explicit responses to the lessons of the data emphasize acts of leadership at every turn: reviewing performance, inquiring about trends and patterns, inviting others to identify solutions. Structures such as the listening system, the assessment calendar, plus/delta, the forecasting chart, and the data road map may prove to be more useful for central office decision makers; the decision matrix, force-field analysis, SWOT/data team analysis, and collaboration checklist may pertain more to classroom teachers. All of the tools offer readers the capacity to increase the quality and quantity of data available to them.

I trust that many of these tools will also equip educators to respond with greater speed and agility to the needs of the students who grace our schools each and every day. The business of education is complex, and although we are more apt to realize our interdependence now than our profession did a decade ago, it is time we discovered how to make data work for us, rather than frenetically chasing elusive test scores without taking the time to find the answers in our midst. *Show Me the Proof!* has been an attempt to provide educators with the tools they need to discover and validate the proof that exists all around them, and to engage one another in making that discovery. I hope that the twenty-three tools in the appendices will also prove to be valuable resources, and I invite readers to share any new tools and insights they develop to leverage antecedents, promote collaboration, and institute accountability. As you do, your efforts will improve the profession, address the needs of all students, and provide evidence to those who ask you to "Show Me the Proof!"

Critical Incident Analysis

Critical incident (Andersen & Fagerhaug, 2000) helps teams understand troublesome symptoms in problematic situations. It is possible that the most careful triangulation of data can fail to reveal patterns that prevent schools and classrooms from moving ahead. Critical incident analysis is fundamentally a group process to systematically and fairly articulate emerging or persistent problems that influence the quality of our efforts to improve student achievement. It is also a prequel for the use of other tools, such as the cause-and-effect fishbone or a relations diagram. It works like this:

1. Assemble a group of participant stakeholders, making sure to include every department or grade level or classification of employee that may be affected by the problem or the challenge to dramatically improve performance or raise student achievement.

2. Ask each participant to respond in writing to one or two predefined questions with as many specifics as possible. Scaffold your request to elicit an incident that:

   a. was most difficult to handle   e. costs the most

                    OR   OR

   b. repeats itself unnecessarily   f. wastes the most time or effort

   c. causes the most problems   g. requires the most re-work
      in completing a *specific*
      assignment/project

                    OR   OR

   d. causes the school embarrassments   h. inhibits student achievement

Select a set of questions that get at the crux of issues that have been resistant to change, slow to improve relative to other district or school efforts, or that keep people from performing at their highest level.

3. Collect the responses and create an affinity chart on which major categories of responses are grouped by responses and presented graphically on chart paper for discussion.

4. Through consensus or use of a decisionmaking matrix, distill the responses down until you identify the most critical incident. Then use that incident as a starting point to identify possible causes and antecedents (Hishakawa Fishbone).

Critical incident analysis uses soft data, not unlike the need for narratives to supplement district or state accountability reports and give the "story behind the numbers" (Reeves, 2004b, 152, 165). It has the capacity to cut through the fog that can cloud a particular challenge, and it is an excellent opportunity to model transparency and a safe learning environment for all. It is recommended here as a fast-track tool to identify improvements that will be relatively easy to implement, and to ensure that observations and perceptions are part of a comprehensive data system.

Collaboration Checklist

Integrating Collaboration into Data Systems	P	I	E	Additional Ways to Integrate Collaboration?
Recommendations are reviewed only when submitted with peers				_____
Collaborative schedules provide common planning and teaming				_____
Teacher teams examine student work before designing interventions				_____
Common assessments are designed, developed, and evaluated by collaborative teams				_____
Leader requests analysis with recommendations for specific students				_____
Assessment calendars establish times for collaboration in analysis, reflection, action planning, and implementation				_____
Early release times are devoted to collaboration around student work				_____
Time and effort are reallocated to respond to urgent challenges as a result of collaboration				_____
Collaborative process selects instructional strategies for each urgent challenge				_____
A data analysis road map is in place				_____
Faculty, department, and grade-level teams systematically engage in collaborative processes to find solutions				_____
Professional development is driven by data on student performance and teaching quality				_____
P = Proposed		I = Introduced		E = Established

Relations Diagram

The main purpose of a relations diagram (Andersen & Fagerhaug, 2000) is to help identify relationships that are not easily recognizable. It is useful in determining relationships among curriculum, specific standards, and subgroup performance patterns. A relations diagram can accommodate up to ten factors.

The following steps describe the process:

1. Determine the factors to be analyzed (events, quantitative data, functions)
2. Place the factors in empty chart boxes
3. Use arrows to illustrate whether factors affect (impact) other factors or are affected (impacted) by them in the relationship
4. Count the arrows to and from each factor

Factors that affect more areas than the number of times they are affected by other factors are *drivers.* Those affected more frequently are *indicators.*

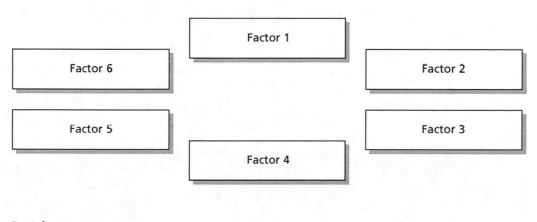

Insights: _____

_____

_____

_____

_____

_____

_____

Next steps: _____

_____

_____

_____

_____

_____

Persons responsible/Reporting date: _____

_____

_____

_____

_____

Assessment
Calendar

Specify times when steps are to be accomplished for each assessment. Use precise dates or windows of time (range of days, months).

Assessment	Administration	Collection Date/Window	Disaggregate Date/Window	Analysis	Reflection	Recommend Changes	Decision Point	Written Rationale	Disseminate to Stakeholders
NRT									
State assessment									
CRTs									
Writing assessment									
EOC assessments									
Common assessments									
Performance assessments									
Unit tests									
Other									

- Scheduled times to collect, aggregate, and disaggregate data
- Required time for analysis, reflection, and recommendations for changes
- Decision points to proceed with status quo or implement change recommendations
- Written rationale for each decision
- Disseminate rationale driven by data to all affected parties

Acts of Accountability

Acts of Accountability	Expected Improvements and Results
Modify time	
Modify opportunities	
Commit resources	
Provide corrective feedback	
Tailor training to needs	
Develop and test hypotheses	
Analyze diverse types of data	
Replicate successful practices	
Make midcourse corrections	
Collaboratively create, implement, and evaluate common assessments	

SWOT/Data Team
Analysis

	Strengths	Weaknesses	Opportunities	Threats
Student performance				
Evidence of teaching				

Insights: _____

_____

_____

_____

_____

_____

_____

Next steps: _____

_____

_____

_____

_____

_____

_____

_____

Persons responsible/Deadline: _____

_____

_____

_____

_____

Scoring Guide Matrix
for Analysis of Data

Data Management

Analysis Dimension	Meeting the Standard	Progressing Toward the Standard	Not Meeting the Standard
Data Collection	The educator makes informed decisions at all levels based on formative assessments of prior learning, embedded assessments during instruction, and summative assessments of results following instruction. Data collection demonstrates understanding of antecedent data, including administrative structures and conditions and cause data (teacher behaviors that engage students in thinking and learning). Results (effects) data includes student performance; pre- and post-data; use of longitudinal cohort data for patterns and trends; embedded performance assessment data; and common assessments by department, grade, or discipline. Data provides evidence of antecedents and instructional strategies. Data collection minimizes interruption of instruction, with data collected limited to critical variables that lend themselves to triangulation.	The educator ensures that teachers and support staff collect and monitor data associated with goals, and that data is maintained for both summative and formative purposes. Emphasis is primarily on collection of results (effects) data, with limited evidence of cause data measures or programmatic and administrative antecedents (conditions and structures that correlate with excellence in student achievement). Educator attempts to schedule data collection so it does not interrupt instruction.	The educator's data collection system is limited to external requirements for compliance in annual student assessment results. No evidence of attempts to link cause and effect; institute continuous assessment measures before, during, and after learning; or address timing issues of data collection.
Improvement Cycles	The educator employs improvement cycles for all major programs and unit teams. Cycles ensure that plans are informed by data, implemented to address gaps and opportunities, analyzed, and routinely and systematically revised for improvement (e.g., 7-step DDDM, PDSA, etc.).	The educator is beginning to apply an improvement cycle to assess student achievement across state or local requirements (e.g., seat time, Carnegie Units, state assessment). Application to adult practices or administrative and programmatic structures has yet to be attempted.	The educator reacts to state or local requirements for data and does not employ improvement cycles that link data to planning and implementation.

Antecedents of Excellence

Analysis Dimension	Meeting the Standard	Progressing Toward the Standard	Not Meeting the Standard
Cause Data and Instructional Strategies	The educator provides evidence of specific antecedents used in classrooms or school to increase student achievement effects (results) through teacher behaviors in the classroom (causes), and systematic teaching strategies. The educator modifies and adjusts antecedent cause data (teaching behaviors and practices), and shares with colleagues current research findings describing causes that produce the greatest gains in student	The educator recognizes effective teaching strategies that impact student thinking and reasoning as causes that lead to achievement effects (results), and is conversant with current research about the causes most apt to produce the greatest gains in student achievement for all subgroups. The educator recognizes that cause/effect data represents strong correlations, not	The educator rarely identifies antecedents or leverages them to increase student achievement.

Antecedents of Excellence (Continued)

Analysis Dimension	Meeting the Standard	Progressing Toward the Standard	Not Meeting the Standard
Cause Data and Instructional Strategies (*Continued*)	achievement for all subgroups; effective cause strategies are implemented in classrooms or the school, and the Hishakawa Fishbone is frequently used to examine current data, determine root causes, and take action through effective intervention plans.	actual causes. The educator is beginning to identify antecedents to improve student achievement based on available data.	
Administrative Structures and Conditions	The educator leverages a wide range of antecedent conditions and structures to increase student achievement, and monitors their impact with user-friendly data. The leader is adept at creating antecedents that increase student achievement, leveraging time, settings, and resources to align and focus efforts (i.e., technological capacity, time and opportunity issues, staff training, levels of implementation in specific teaching strategies, attendance).	The educator recognizes antecedents in terms of time, technology, training, logistics, and level of implementation, and applies them periodically to improve student achievement based on external research findings and antecedents employed in neighboring or comparable schools.	The educator does not view administrative structures of time, technology, textbooks, or training as possible antecedents for excellence that can be modified for improved student achievement.

Collaboration around Student Work

Planning to Execution	The educator ensures ongoing, reflective, and meaningful collaboration that captures the best thinking of staff to improve student achievement through a variety of methods, such as: (1) **action planning**, including all steps of a continuous improvement cycle; (2) **lesson logs** shared and distributed by departments or grade-level teams; (3) **common assessments** created, evaluated, and revised by teacher teams; (4) **instructional calendars** that align curriculum and instruction with regent examinations; (5) development of **data teams** to monitor outlier student performance and close learning gaps, or (6) establishment of a clearly defined **program evaluation** process. Teacher-developed measures of collaboration complement those initiated by individual educator.	The educator promotes collaboration around student work by examining student work at faculty meetings and asking staff to identify solutions to patterns of lagging student achievement and strategies to replicate evidence of dramatically improving student achievement. The educator promotes collaborative data analysis by establishing one or more ongoing methods to examine student performance and implement strategies to improve that performance: (1) **lesson logs** shared and distributed by departments or grade-level teams; (2) **common assessments** created, evaluated, and revised by teacher teams; or (3) **instructional calendars** that align curriculum and instruction with regent examinations.	The educator looks for the path of least resistance in developing data monitoring systems; she or he frequently avoids collaboration beyond initial consensus to adopt a program or strategy; reflection is nonexistent.

(continues)

Collaboration around Student Work *(Continued)*

Analysis Dimension	Meeting the Standard	Progressing Toward the Standard	Not Meeting the Standard
Team Thinking	Solutions generated by others are valued, especially when generated from within the educator's support group. The leader ensures that team thinking permeates the data analysis process by requiring that: (1) all team members proactively analyze data for discussion in advance of meetings; (2) team processes routinely identify improvements; (3) training is provided and encouraged in mental models, team learning, and cognitive coaching; and (4) training updates on data analysis tools are provided to all teams.	The educator promotes team thinking in data analysis by providing and encouraging: (1) training in mental models, team learning, and cognitive coaching; and (2) training in data analysis tools for interested team members.	There is no evidence of a systematic plan to improve the quality of collaborative thinking in examining student work.
Integration into Decision Making	The educator integrates collaboration in data analysis into all key decisions through collaborative processes that benefit from the best thinking of classroom teachers. Evidence is demonstrated through a variety of means, such as: (1) recommendations are reviewed only when submitted with peers; (2) collaborative schedules provide common planning, teaming; (3) teacher teams examine student work; leader requests analysis and recommendations for specific students; (4) assessment calendars are required of all department/grade-level teams; (5) early release times are established for collaboration around student work; (6) time and effort are reallocated to respond to urgent challenges, through collaboration that develops powerful instructional strategies. Assessment calendars establish times for collaboration in analysis, reflection, action planning, and implementation.	The educator attempts to integrate collaboration in data analysis into decision making by one or more of the following: (1) requesting that recommendations be submitted with support by two other peers; (2) establishing school schedules with common planning/teaming; or (3) providing data to teacher teams (flexible grouping) and requesting analysis and recommendations for specific students.	The educator views decisions regarding data analysis as the prerogative of administration or as isolated acts of leadership separate from lessons revealed by data.

Accountability

Analysis Dimension	Meeting the Standard	Progressing Toward the Standard	Not Meeting the Standard
Authority to Act	The educator establishes written policies, within his or her direct control and influence, that provide teachers and other staff the authority to implement changes designed to improve student achievement based on a preponderance of the evidence revealed	The educator advocates for written policies, within his or her direct control and influence, that provide teachers and other staff the authority to implement changes designed to improve student achievement.	The educator defers to popular opinion in making changes, with little evidence of efforts to extend authority for program or

Accountability *(Continued)*

Analysis Dimension	Meeting the Standard	Progressing Toward the Standard	Not Meeting the Standard
Authority to Act *(Continued)*	from data available at any given time. Preponderance of evidence is determined through triangulation of data and thoughtful collaboration around actual student performance.	Data provides some evidence to assist teachers and staff in making changes designed to improve student achievement; triangulation and thoughtful collaboration occur sporadically among teachers and staff.	instructional changes to teachers or staff.
Accountability Structures	The educator integrates accountability into all major decisions by delineating explicit responsibilities for teams and individuals, establishing user-friendly timelines for data, and establishes multiple feedback systems, such as assessment calendars, formal listening systems for student, teacher, parent, and staff stakeholder groups, grade level/department teams, or data teams.	The educator has developed accountability methods that specify responsibilities for teams and individuals, establish timelines for data collection/disaggregation, and provide at least one formal and responsive feedback system to improve student achievement.	Focus is on compliance with external requirements established by supervisor or institutional policy; little evidence exists to demonstrate a commitment or plan to add value with accountability systems.
Accountability Reports	The educator publicly displays and communicates results of ongoing, monitored accountability measures for Tier 1 data (system-wide indicators), Tier 2 data (school-based indicators), and Tier 3 data (narrative description of school successes and challenges). The educator supplements measures at all levels with performance indicators that add value and focus efforts to improve student achievement.	The educator communicates the results of ongoing, monitored accountability measures that exceed Tier 1 (district-wide indicators) requirements, and supplements such measures with a number of performance indicators that add value and focus efforts to improve student achievement.	The educator communicates only those results mandated by external requirements (Tier 1 or compliance measures). There is no evidence of plans to develop, monitor, or communicate Tier 2 or Tier 3 data to staff, parents, students, or patrons.
Permission to Subtract	The leader establishes written policies, within his or her direct control and influence, that give teachers and other staff permission to eliminate, reduce, or omit historical practices or instructional strategies that inhibit improved student achievement, based on a preponderance of the evidence revealed from data available at any given time. Preponderance of evidence is determined through deliberate triangulation of data and thoughtful collaboration around actual student performance.	The leader has developed a policy giving teachers and staff permission to eliminate, reduce, or omit historical practices or instructional strategies that inhibit improved student achievement, but has yet to establish written policies, within his or her direct control and influence, to that effect, and has not yet developed a system to monitor implementation of the policy. Data provides some evidence of assistance to teachers and staff in eliminating obsolete, redundant, or neutral practices that do not contribute to improved student achievement. Triangulation and thoughtful collaboration around student performance occur sporadically among teachers and staff.	The leader is reluctant to share the authority to eliminate, reduce, or omit existing practices with staff, and is unable to identify current instructional strategies or antecedents (conditions and structures) that inhibit improved student achievement for groups or individuals.

(continues)

Accountability (*Continued*)

Analysis Dimension	Meeting the Standard	Progressing Toward the Standard	Not Meeting the Standard
Responsibility for Results	Performance goals are met for student achievement that meet AYP requirements and close the learning gap for all subgroups. Sustained record of improved student achievement on multiple indicators of student success can be verified. Explicit use of previous and interim data indicates a focus on improving performance. Efforts to assist students who demonstrate proficiency to move to the advanced or exemplary level are evident, and new challenges are met by identification of needs from existing data, creation of timely and effective interventions with monitoring data, and selection of meaningful and insightful results indicators.	Staff members report that they should be responsible for student achievement results, but have limited understanding of the factors (antecedents) that effect student achievement. There is evidence of improvement for one or more subgroups, but insufficient evidence of changes in antecedent measures of teaching, curriculum, and leadership to create the improvements necessary to achieve student performance goals for all subgroups.	Indifferent to the data; tendency to blame students, families, and external characteristics. Staff and leaders do not believe that student achievement can improve through their efforts. No evidence of decisive action to change time, teacher assignments, curriculum, leadership practices, or other variables of achievement.

Analysis Methods

Analysis Dimension	Meeting the Standard	Progressing Toward the Standard	Not Meeting the Standard
Continuous Improvement	The leader has established a continuous improvement framework that includes flowcharting for all major procedures in the school and in classrooms, use of control charts to monitor areas where zero tolerance is required, and monitoring of cycle time from planning to implementation. Teachers are given authority to commit resources within their classrooms to modify practices to respond to achievement data and meet individual needs. The leader monitors the presence of antecedents as part of the observation process. The leader has empowered teachers and staff to examine their work routines and habits with analysis tools such as flowcharting, relations diagrams, and gap analysis. Analysis method answers the question: How can we improve daily routines and sustain innovation for improved student achievement?	The leader encourages teachers to modify their practices and engage students in modifying their practices in the classroom. The leader asks staff to identify areas where effort is duplicated to find ways to redirect time and effort.	The leader attempts to improve the ability to meet deadlines and complete reports on time without inaccuracies or typographical errors. Little time is devoted to improvement of instructional practices to increase student achievement.

Analysis Methods (Continued)

Analysis Dimension	Meeting the Standard	Progressing Toward the Standard	Not Meeting the Standard
Analysis Selection	The leader routinely matches the purpose for examining data with the analysis tool before analyzing data or developing solutions and plans. The leader trains staff to recognize the relationship between purpose and analysis method. A defined process ensures that systems analysis, problem solving, decision making, clarification analysis, action research, and continuous improvement are used as appropriate.	The leader examines data to inform decisions, and summarizes results with charts and graphs. There is some evidence of how analysis informs decisions.	The leader complies with require-ments to collect and disaggregate data, but there is little evidence of analysis that informs decisions; tradition and perceptions trump data and facts in the analysis process.
Systems Analysis	The leader understands the purpose of systems analysis and employs appropriate tools to gather data that reveals the level of interdependence and the degree to which unintended consequences result. The leader trains staff to examine parts, functions, and relationships within systems, and has a defined process to examine key subsystems in schools (e.g., leadership systems, planning and strategy systems, listening systems, information and data systems, the work environment, work habits, and performance and process results). Analysis method answers the question: How do I examine purpose, parts, and functions, and identify gaps?	The leader understands the purpose of systems analysis and employs apropriate tools to gather data that reveals the leve of interdependence and the degree to which unintended consequences result.	The leader is unaware of the inte·dependent nature of compre-hensive schools and discovers unintended consequences accidentally rather than through deliberate examination of data.
Problem Solving	The leader uses problem-solving analysis to find the best possible solution or path to achieve goals. The leader employs data tools with assistance and input from staff to find the most effective solution to challenges and achieve organizational goals given existing barriers, challenges, and opportunities. Tools including Venn diagrams, force-field analysis, and critical incident analysis are used to pursue ambitious and challenging goals in light of realistic challenges and potential barriers. Analysis method answers the question: How can we achieve goals with current barriers and constraints?	The leader uses problem-solving analysis to select the best possible solution, and considers barriers and challenges to achieving organizational goals when developing action plans and strategies.	The leader sees little relationship between goals and problems, engaging in planning that seldom anticipates problems or challenges and tends to pursue only the safest goals.

(continues)

Analysis Methods *(Continued)*

Analysis Dimension	Meeting the Standard	Progressing Toward the Standard	Not Meeting the Standard
Decision Making	The leader engages staff in the use of decisionmaking analysis to set priorities, choosing the best alternative action on the basis of established criteria and values. Procedures are established to ensure that priorities flow from an established procedure and a common matrix is utilized for all major decisions. Analysis method answers the question: How should we set priorities?	The leader uses decisionmaking analysis to set priorities, choosing the best alternative action on the basis of established criteria and values. The leader has begun to formalize a decisionmaking process and engage staff and faculty in its development and implementation.	The leader sees little relationship between priorities and data analysis, engaging in decisions based on tradition and very seldom considering alternatives.
Clarification	The leader routinely engages staff and faculty in clarification analysis to reduce confusion by identifying the underlying issue, establishing known and agreed-upon facts surrounding the issue, and specifying the areas of contradiction that are the basis of existing confusion. The leader facilitates a collaborative process that leads to resolution and clarification at all levels. Analysis method answers the question: How can we clarify to reduce confusion?	The leader uses clarification analysis to reduce confusion by identifying the underlying issue, establishing known and agreed-upon facts surrounding the issue, and specifying the areas of contradiction that are the basis of existing confusion. The leader is beginning to include staff and faculty in the process.	The leader is unaware of the need for clarification, and typically implements new programs with inadequate preparation or training for staff and faculty.
Action Research as Analysis	The leader routinely engages teachers in action research to verify, validate, and replicate effective teaching practices. The leader has made action research available to teachers when patterns suggest strong relationships that result in improved student achievement. Analysis method answers the question: How do we translate local data into viable innovation for possible replication?	The leader routinely pursues hunches about relationships between instructional strategies, antecedent conditions, and student achievement that are indicated in data that has been analyzed. The leader is considering making action research available to teachers when patterns suggest strong relationships that result in improved student achievement.	The leader does not engage in action research and views associated data collection as interfering with instruction and attention to students.

Triangulation

Analysis Dimension	Meeting the Standard	Progressing Toward the Standard	Not Meeting the Standard
Triangulation	The educator applies at least two data tools to every triangulation, triangulating student achievement data effectively with supporting student achievement data, antecedent data (conditions and structure), accountability data (responsibilities, reporting, SMART measures), or collaboration data (various team formats, lesson logs, instructional calendars, etc.). The educator monitors staff triangulation of achievement data to ensure inclusion of related and unrelated data points (e.g., instructional strategies, allocation of time, professional development, side-by-side curriculum analysis, standards, and assessments).	The educator applies at least one data tool to every triangulation effort, and is beginning to triangulate student achievement data with antecedents, collaboration data, or accountability structures (principles of DDDM).	The educator is unaware of the principle of triangulation of data, and instead focuses his or her efforts on compliance with district and state reports.
Low Inference Insights	The educator leverages triangulation to engage teachers in self-discovery of insights, new learning, and recommendations for changes in the educational process. The educator triangulates data effectively, with each point serving as a check on the other dimensions; the desired outcome is the realization of new insights from the various data points (and types) that are not available from examining one type of data or one perspective in isolation.	The educator understands that triangulation requires teams to make assumptions, draw inferences, and come to conclusions without total certainty. The educator recognizes that triangulation necessitates discovery of a center point from other, often unrelated data, and the educator triangulates student assessment data with antecedents and cause data wherever possible.	The educator is directive in interactions with teachers, and does not engage teachers in triangulation of data.
Triangulation Conversations	The educator models triangulation in formal and informal settings, and asks teachers to add value to their analysis of all data by triangulating data with colleagues. Triangulation is an expected exercise for all grade, department, and data team meetings, and the leader routinely includes cause data and administrative antecedents in triangulation. The educator applies triangulation to encourage innovative teaching strategies and facilitate new approaches to instruction through action research. Data is specifically analyzed to engage staff in conversations about assessments.	The educator uses the triangulation process to coach teachers in making assumptions, drawing inferences, and developing hunches that can help identify replicable practices, verified through action research.	The educator views data as numbers and does not engage faculty or staff in making inferences or reaching for assumptions, believing that none of the school staff is a statistician and shouldn't claim to be.

(continues)

115

Replication

Analysis Dimension	Meeting the Standard	Progressing Toward the Standard	Not Meeting the Standard
Replication	The educator has a system in place to identify home-grown successes that includes a common definition, a process to recognize successes, and a method to validate and replicate the successful practice. The educator has defined a preponderance of evidence as sufficient data to answer the questions: What works well for whom, why, and how do you know?	The educator promotes replication of best practices from current educational research and has a system in place to recognize teachers for improved student achievement. At least one replication is discussed and teachers are encouraged to observe each other for best practices.	The educator resists efforts to formally replicate practices, viewing the process as divisive and as singling out one teacher over another.
Decision to Replicate	The educator follows up on hunches associated with data patterns by initiating a process for replication with teachers when student performance patterns correlate with specific strategies or antecedent structures and conditions for learning. The educator employs a specific decisionmaking process at key intervals with affected teachers to determine how, when, and whether to replicate a practice.	The educator communicates frequently with teachers to identify patterns and trends in student performance that correlate with specific instructional strategies or the presence of antecedent structures and conditions for learning. The leader initiates a discussion about possible replication with affected teachers and staff.	The educator views differences in classroom performance as inherent differences in teaching personality and student demographics.
Action Research	The educator is fluent in the six steps of action research, and is quick to translate hunches about patterns into action research hypotheses, engaging teachers and staff in a common action research approach characterized by: ■ 1:1 relationship design between independent variable (cause data) and dependent variable (effect) ■ Simple pre/post assessments ■ Use of same course/grade classrooms as control group ■ Effective teaching strategies as independent variables ■ Data collection embedded into instruction ■ Prescribed time period, format	The educator is fluent in the six steps of action research: 1. Observe 2. Explain 3. Predict 4. Test hypothesis 5. Gather data 6. Explain The educator examines data for patterns and trends associated with specific classrooms and instructional strategies.	The educator shows no interest in action research, viewing the time and effort required to implement it as disruptive to the learning process.

Leadership in Data Analysis

Analysis Dimension	Meeting the Standard	Progressing Toward the Standard	Not Meeting the Standard
Explicit Acts of Leadership	The leader has established a set of behaviors that set expectations, monitor performance, communicate values, and promote vision in data analysis. Evidence is available of intentional, explicit acts of leadership in data analysis to improve student achievement, including evidence of how the leader: ■ Examines components of systems ■ Generates the best available solution to achieve a goal or resolve a specific problem ■ Sets priorities from a list of alternatives ■ Reduces confusion regarding a current program or eliminates an obsolete practice ■ Replicates an innovation based on local data ■ Improves routines, protocols, or procedures to increase achievement or staff efficiency.	The leader is able to provide some evidence of intentional, explicit acts of leadership in data analysis to improve student achievement (i.e., leader employs a decisionmaking process that engages faculty in setting priorities annually, with revision and updating at monthly faculty meetings). Leader is beginning to develop a set of behaviors that set expectations, monitor performance, communicate values, and promote vision.	The leader focuses time and energy on completing management task requirements for compliance at her or his school. No evidence is available to indicate that the leader sets expectations, monitors performance, communicates values, or promotes vision in terms of data analysis.
Candor	The leader actively encourages collaboration and input from others in generating solutions. The leader is not afraid to be humble, and is cognizant of the human environment in which he or she operates. The leader values the collective total as greater than an individual contribution and investigates interim solutions. The leader has established a formal listening system to promote a culture of candor.	The leader enlists input from parents, teachers, students, and patrons to inform planning and improve student achievement. The leader responds to school community feedback (which is primarily traditional satisfaction surveys) with limited feedback regarding instructional strategies, teacher behavior (cause data), or antecedents in terms of conditions and structures for learning.	The leader complies with minimal institutional requirements, communicating positive outcome data and justifying the status quo. The leader has very limited understanding of causes of student achievement.
Habits of Work	The leader systematically examines how time and effort are expended in the school and in classrooms to identify processes that contribute to improved student achievement (antecedents), processes that do not contribute to improved student achievement, and processes that are not as efficient as possible.	The leader periodically identifies work habits that should be revised to reduce duplication of effort, improve efficiency, and focus efforts to improve student achievement. The leader conducts analysis using data tools, and schedules planned changes.	The leader views work habits as separate from the instructional process, and values compliance with existing procedures above improvement of such procedures.

(continues)

117

Leadership in Data Analysis (*Continued*)

Analysis Dimension	Meeting the Standard	Progressing Toward the Standard	Not Meeting the Standard
Habits of Work (*Continued*)	The leader empowers teachers to modify their practices and engage their students in modifying their own work habits through the use of a wide range of analysis tools. The leader not only identifies work habits that should be revised to reduce duplication of effort, improve efficiency, and improve student achievement, but also takes immediate action to improve their effect in both instructional and support processes.		
Listening Systems	The leader ensures that listening systems provide multiple opportunities for stakeholder feedback throughout the school year (e.g., Web sites, focus groups, surveys). Systems ensure that the data collected is acted upon in a timely manner and that authority to commit resources is provided to teachers and staff. All listening systems are cyclical, predictable in timing and format, public (open, transparent), and user-friendly, and the leader models openness by communicating criticisms and suggested changes with as much enthusiasm as accolades and success reports.	The leader has established a listening system that gathers satisfaction data from parents, teachers, staff, students, and community patrons. Data is analyzed at least annually, with results and recommendations included in the school improvement planning process.	The leader complies with district and state requirements for communication with survey stakeholders. Results are seldom used to generate changes in instruction, curriculum, or creation of responsive antecedents.
Data Presentations	The leader has provided training in presentation guidelines that teachers and staff adhere to, including describing data in its context (Tier 3 data), and has established scaling guidelines to avoid skewing of data. The leader fosters a conservative approach to interpretation, avoidance of conjecture, liberal use of graphic organizers, and a focus on big ideas, trends and patterns in presentation.	The leader personally follows presentation guidelines, but has yet to provide training and structure for teachers and faculty. The leader adheres to guidelines for context, scaling, interpretation, and focuses on big ideas, trends, and patterns. Presentations are detailed and communicate appropriately to all audiences.	The leader attempts to make the data look good by skewing scales, using anecdotal evidence to discount or embellish data, and frequent conjecturing about findings. Presentations tend to use detailed and complex charts or graphs, and show little attention to the big ideas or links with current and future planning.

Leadership in Data Analysis (Continued)

Analysis Dimension	Meeting the Standard	Progressing Toward the Standard	Not Meeting the Standard
Urgency Response	The leader includes urgency as a critical component of the decisionmaking process by projecting the impact of data trends in student achievement, funding, demographic changes, and staff changes in terms of external mandates and internal goal targets. The leader serves staff by routinely including such projections at faculty meetings and seminars, and inviting analysis, problem solving, and reflection from participating staff.	The leader periodically presents data projections in student achievement to staff and faculty; trends other than student achievement have yet to be analyzed.	The leader seldom examines the impact of data trends in any area, and frequently misses opportunities for dialogue about challenges that invite an urgent response.
Assessment Calendar	The leader ensures that there are defined procedures for collecting, analyzing, reflecting on, and acting on data, including scheduled times to collect, aggregate, and disaggregate data. Times are scheduled for analysis, reflection, and communication of recommendations. The leader establishes decision points to proceed, maintain the status quo, or implement changes following data analysis. The leader insists on written rationales for key school and classroom decisions, and disseminates the rationales for decisions driven by data to all affected parties.	The leader collects, analyzes, and reflects on data before determining a course of action. The leader is beginning to formalize the process and set aside times for analysis, reflection, and communication of recommendations. Decisions are not reduced to writing, and the leader seldom disseminates data-based rationales for key decisions to affected parties.	The leader communicates data required by state and district reports and includes some charts and graphs in the annual report. There is no systematic process for communicating data.

A Data Road Map

A *data plan road map* is designed to reveal areas where improvement has been lacking or growth stagnant, and where efforts have failed to produce results. *Drive carefully!*

1. Intersections

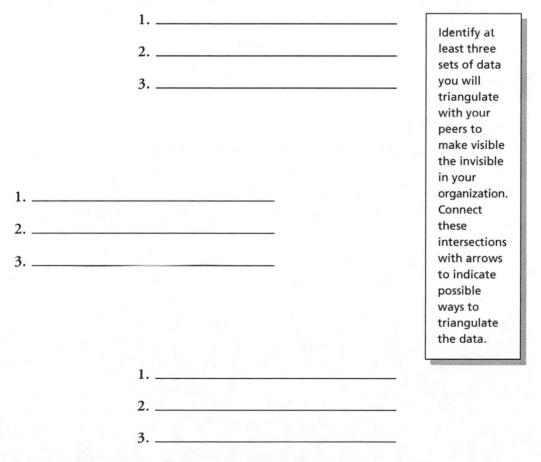

1. _____

2. _____

3. _____

1. _____

2. _____

3. _____

Identify at least three sets of data you will triangulate with your peers to make visible the invisible in your organization. Connect these intersections with arrows to indicate possible ways to triangulate the data.

1. _____

2. _____

3. _____

2. Data Driving Habits

To Change	To Increase	To Improve	To Create

3. Rearview-Mirror Effects

Headlights: Proactive Strategies for Looking Forward

1. _____

   _____ (beginning __/__/200_)

2. _____

   _____ (beginning __/__/200_)

3. _____

   _____ (beginning __/__/200_)

4. _____

   _____ (beginning __/__/200_)

Canaries for Your Classroom

1. _____
   _____ (beginning __/__/200_)

2. _____
   _____ (beginning __/__/200_)

3. _____
   _____ (beginning __/__/200_)

4. _____
   _____ (beginning __/__/200_)

Canaries for Your School

1. _____
   _____ (beginning __/__/200_)

2. _____
   _____ (beginning __/__/200_)

3. _____
   _____ (beginning __/__/200_)

4. _____
   _____ (beginning __/__/200_)

Canaries for Your District

1. _____
   _____ (beginning __/__/200_)

2. _____
   _____ (beginning __/__/200_)

3. _____
   _____ (beginning __/__/200_)

4. _____
   _____ (beginning __/__/200_)

4. Traffic Signals and Signs (Feedback Systems)

To Change	To Increase	To Improve	To Create
By __/__/200_	By __/__/200_	By __/__/200_	By __/__/200_

5. Detours and Road Closures

Practices to Subtract	Policies to Subtract	Programs/Organizational Structures to Subtract
By __/__/200_	By __/__/200_	By __/__/200_

6. Use Your Digital Camera (User-Friendly Embedded Data)

Snapshot Data—Students	Frequency	Snapshot Data—Adults	Frequency

Snapshot Data—Administrative Structures	Frequency	Snapshot Data—Time and Opportunity	Frequency

7. Data in Action: Explicit Changes in Our DDDM System (Collection, Communication, Calendar)

The Data of Teaching: What Adults Do

To Change	To Increase	To Improve	To Create
By __/__/200_	By __/__/200_	By __/__/200_	By __/__/200_

The Data of Learning: Evidence of Thinking (Bloom's Taxonomy)

To Change	To Increase	To Improve	To Create
By __/__/200_	By __/__/200_	By __/__/200_	By __/__/200_

The Data of Improving: Doing What We Do Now, Only Better

To Change	To Increase	To Improve	To Create
By __/__/200_	By __/__/200_	By __/__/200_	By __/__/200_

The Data of Persuading

Trends to Establish	Patterns to Examine	Benchmarks to Achieve	Strengths to Celebrate
By __/__/200_	By __/__/200_	By __/__/200_	By __/__/200_

8. Building Your Superhighway (Leadership)

Strategies to Build Team Thinking	Strategies to Release Authority to Commit Resources	Strategies to Grant Permission to Stop

The Data Road Map

School: _____ School Year: _____

Data Team: _____

	Implementation Timeline		
	Start	**Evaluate**	**Complete**

Intersections
- ☐ Triangulation 1
- ☐ Triangulation 2
- ☐ Triangulation 3

Data Driving Habits
- ☐ To Change
- ☐ To Increase
- ☐ To Improve
- ☐ To Create

Rearview-Mirror Effects
- ☐ Improve the Headlights
- ☐ Canaries for the Classroom
- ☐ Canaries for the School
- ☐ Canaries for the System

Traffic Signals and Signs
- ☐ Feedback System Changes
- ☐ Listening System Changes

Detours and Road Closures
- ☐ Practices to Subtract
- ☐ Policies to Subtract
- ☐ Structures to Subtract

Use Your Digital Camera:
Catch the Scenery
- ☐ Student Data
- ☐ Adult Data

Implementation Timeline *(Continued)*

	Start	Evaluate	Complete

Use Your Digital Camera:
Catch the Scenery *(Continued)*

❑ Structure Data

❑ Time and Opportunity Data

Data in Action

❑ Teaching

❑ Learning

❑ Improving

❑ Persuading

Building Your Superhighway
(Leadership)

❑ Team Thinking

❑ Agility in Committing Resources

❑ Permission to Stop

Summary: _____

_____

_____

_____

_____

_____

_____

APPENDIX

Data Analysis
and Principles

Analysis Method	Purpose	Existing Data	Antecedents—Specific Behaviors/Strategies Implemented/Planned	Collaboration—Structures Implemented/Planned	Accountability—Structures Implemented/Planned

Flowcharting

Flowcharting Components. Flowcharts are key to continuous improvement analyses. They help clarify sequences, process steps, instructional protocols, and policy implementation. Deployment flowcharts are useful tools for managing projects from planning to completion when time is critical. Flowcharts provide the means to recognize and respond to duplication of effort, eliminate inefficiencies, and identify fragmented efforts unrelated to goals. A template for deployment of an assessment calendar is provided, with two popular examples.

Flowchart Components

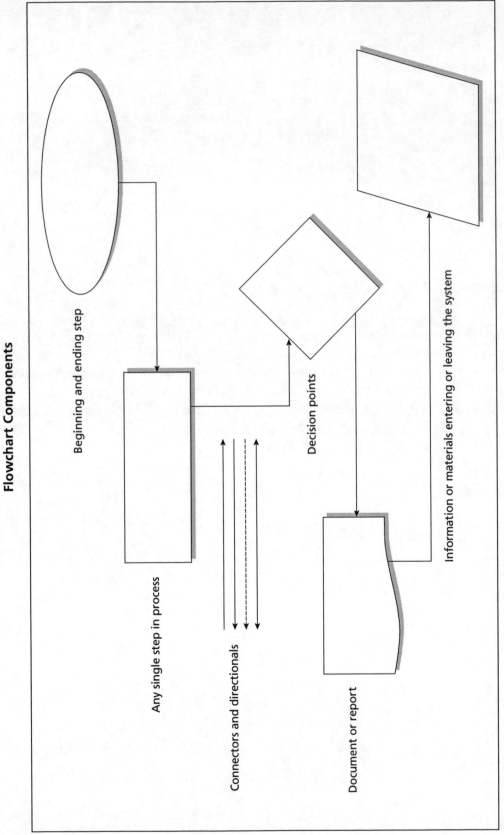

Beginning and ending step

Any single step in process

Connectors and directionals

Decision points

Document or report

Information or materials entering or leaving the system

Deployment Flowchart and Assessment Calendar Interface

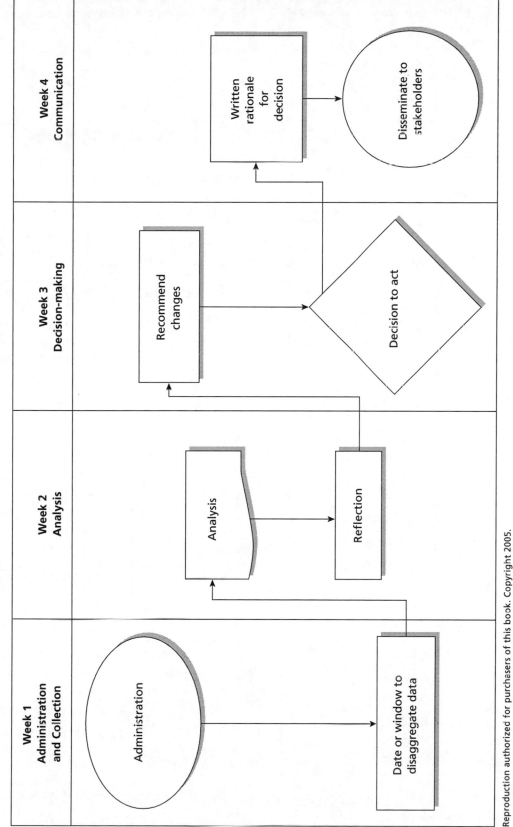

Flowchart and Process Map Path to Excellence

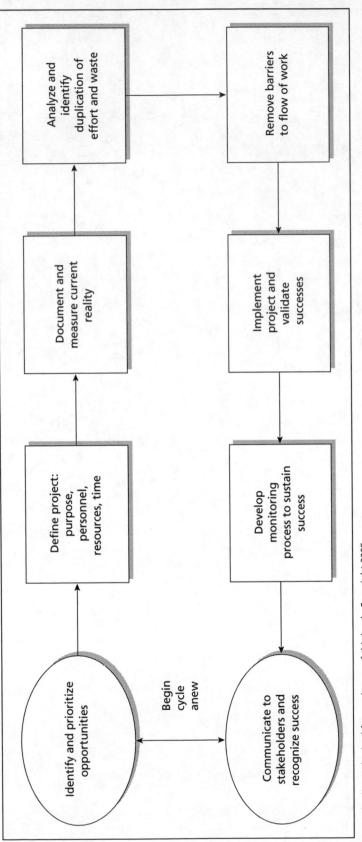

Venn Diagram

Recommended Design

Dependent variable in center

- Antecedents in A
- Collaboration activities in B
- Accountability structures in C

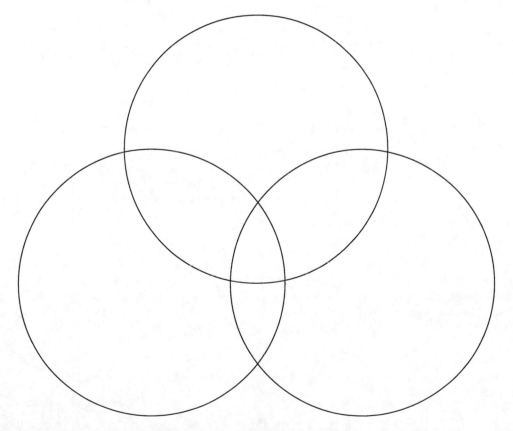

Considerations for Creating Venn Diagrams

- What do I know about this situation?
- What are the three most important elements of this situation?
- What characteristics do the elements have in common?
- What characteristics do the elements not have in common?

Force-Field Analysis

1. Select problem from systems analysis tools (fishbone, 5 Ws, flowchart, critical incident) and write narrative of problem, including context. (How long has problem existed? Have there been other attempts to eliminate, mitigate?)

2. Describe barriers in terms of forces preventing resolution of problem.

3. Describe possible ways to overcome barriers as possible solutions.

4. Select solutions that best address specific elements of the problem.

Problem, Challenge, and/or Goal	Persistent Barriers

Major Barriers (Reduce from Upper Right Quadrant)	High Likelihood Solutions/Strategies/Interventions

Decision Matrix

		Alternatives (range of scores =)		
Criteria	**Weight**	**#1**	**#2**	**#3**
1.				
2.				
3.				
4.				
5.				
6.				
7.				
8.				
9.				
10.				

Criteria = What is valued/weighted
Range = Low to high scores
Scores = Range × Weight

Clarification
Analysis

Area requiring clarification:

Essence of issue: (Q.)

Known or agreed upon:	Areas of confusion/contradictions:

Resolution:

APPENDIX

Triangulation

Template for Triangulation of Data

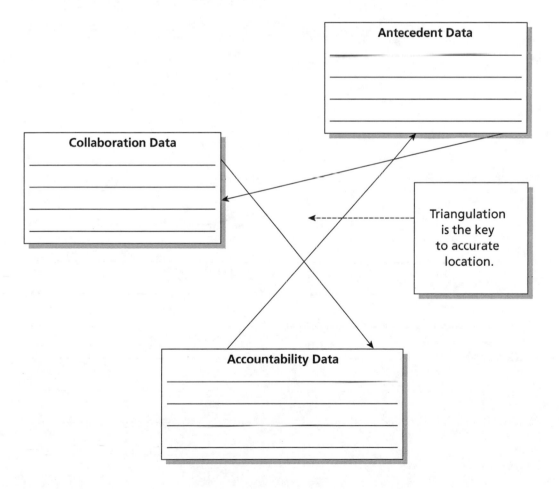

What do we **Know** from these data? (patterns, trends, similarities, differences, outliers)

_____

_____

_____

_____

_____

_____

What do we **Want** to find out? (decide on purpose of analysis)

_____

_____

_____

_____

_____

_____

What do we need to **Learn,** and how will we know we learned it? (choose analysis method)

_____

_____

_____

_____

_____

_____

Wagon-Wheel

Steps in Using Wagon Wheels

1. Assign key variables to each spoke on wheel (10).

2. Collect data across key variables.

3. Establish scale for each spoke, with highest performance on outer rim of circle. Label each individual spoke with its own scale.

4. Plot performance data along spokes, color-coding to distinguish units being compared (classrooms, schools, departments, grade levels, budgets, certification areas, etc.).

5. Connect lines for each unit if comparisons are made between units.

6. Identify the pattern of performance against selected performance standards.

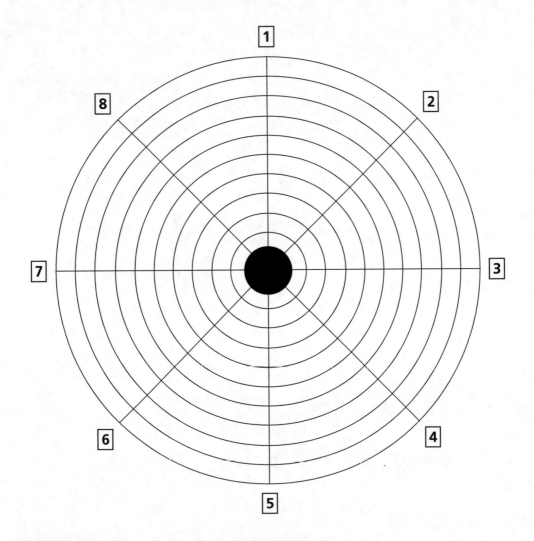

Wagon-Wheel Tool for Data Analysis

School: _____ Date: _____

Department/Team: _____

_____

Team Members: _____

_____

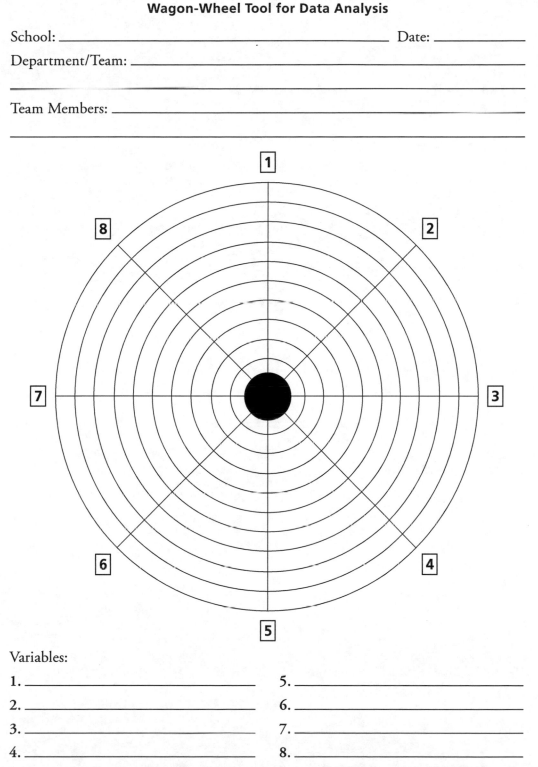

Variables:

1. _____   5. _____

2. _____   6. _____

3. _____   7. _____

4. _____   8. _____

The Hishakawa Fishbone: A Cause-and-Effect Diagram

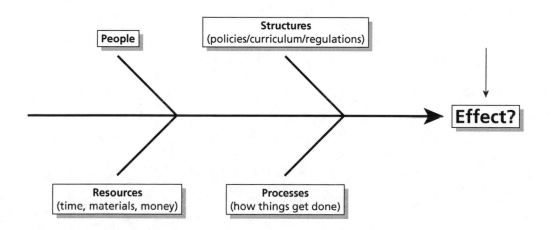

Tips for Cause–Effect Analyses

1. Brainstorm for possible causes of the effect or problem.
2. Assign possible causes to basic categories.
3. Use responses to "why?" questions as branches to causes.
4. Look for causes that appear repeatedly.
5. Reach consensus.
6. Gather data to determine the relative impact of causes.
7. Develop an action plan to address the cause at its root.

Group Norms
for Meetings and
Data Analysis

Meeting Norms	Data Analysis Norms
<ul><li>Be on time and work as a team</li><li>Respect confidentiality at all times</li><li>Be open and honest in communication</li><li>Respect the speaker and be willing to disagree agreeably</li><li>Understand the other person's point of view before expressing your own</li><li>Keep comments simple and straightforward</li><li>Suspend judgment regarding suggestions for change until topic is thoroughly discussed, researched, reviewed</li><li>Learn and share at every meeting</li><li>Maintain a sense of humor</li><li>Close with a +/Δ to continually improve meeting effectiveness</li></ul>	<ul><li>Establish meeting norms and reduce them to writing</li><li>Diversity of ideas: Don't meet without them</li><li>Homework: Come prepared to teach</li><li>Roles to elicit candor: Make sure no stone (gem) is left unturned</li><li>Numbers yield hunches: Don't leave meetings without one</li><li>Tools are to use. Acquire and build competency in use of analysis tools</li><li>Publish and disseminate meeting results</li></ul>
Adopted Meeting Norms	**Adopted Data Analysis Norms**

Adopted Meeting Norms *(Continued)*	Adopted Data Analysis Norms *(Continued)*

Control, Run, and Discrepancy Charts

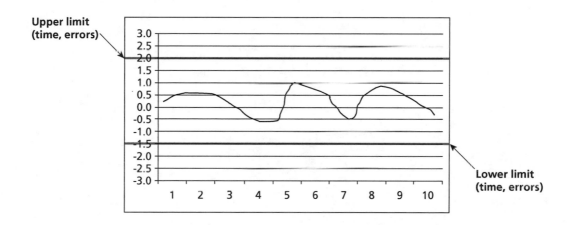

Control, Run, or Discrepancy Charts

A control chart or discrepancy chart is desirable when you wish to have as little variance as possible. Lesson plans devoted to specific power standards or subscales where the school or cohort group needs considerable improvement are examples of possible **control charts.** A common method of establishing an acceptable range for control charts is to calculate (1) average scores of the population as the lower limit and (2) a trend line from current averages to desired outcome within the given time frame. Then establish a targeted upper limit, outside of which would be considered a benchmark performance worthy of replication. Control charts give monitors of performance an early warning—the educational equivalent of the "canary in the coal mine." They are often constructed to achieve AYP gain requirements of the NCLB Act.

Discrepancy charts measure deviation from a preferred standard, such as when you want to measure time devoted to a particular standard or deficit area requiring more intensive instruction. In this case, the lower limit would be the minimal acceptable time devoted to teach the standard; the upper limit would be the maximum allowable time devoted. The example is a discrepancy chart.

Whereas control and run charts may use any scale, discrepancy charts measure deviation from a desired standard. **Run charts** merely measure frequencies over time to monitor fluctuations, such as tardies on given days (Mondays, Fridays, homecoming, etc.).

Side-by-Side
Analysis

Side-by-Side Analysis of Curriculum, Assessments, Standards, and Data Tools

	Test Performance	Common Assessment Performance	Standards Addressed	Curriculum: Level/Grade/Course/Unit	Analysis Tool(s)
Population					
Subgroup					
Student					
Population					
Subgroup					
Student					
Population					
Subgroup					
Student					
Population					
Subgroup					
Student					

Findings from triangulation (patterns, gaps) _____

Conclusion and decision _____

Key to Analysis Tools Abbreviations:

Celeration chart	Cel	Flowchart	F	Relations diagram	R
Control chart	Con	Force-field analysis	FF	Triangulation	T
Critical incident	CI	Hishakawa Fishbone	C/E	Venn diagram	V
Discrepancy chart	D	Plus/Delta	Δ	Wagon-wheel chart	WW

Listening System

Part I: Stakeholder Satisfaction

School: _____ Principal: _____ Date: _____ Email: _____

Stakeholder Surveys	Parents	Teachers and Administrators	Staff	Students	Patrons	P	I	E	Rationale: Current Practice
What do we currently do with the data?									
Authority to act? (commit resources)									
Who?/When?									
How?									
Summary of Stakeholder Satisfaction Listening Systems:									

P = Proposed   I = Introduced   E = Established
Guidelines for listening systems: Cyclical, predictable, public (open, transparent), user-friendly

Part II: Focus Groups and Structured Interviews

School: _____   Principal: _____   Date: _____   Email: _____

Focus Groups and Structured Interviews	Parents	Teachers and Administrators	Staff	Students	Patrons	P	I	E	Rationale: Current Practice
What do we currently do with the data?									
Authority to act? (commit resources)									
Who?/When?									
How?									

Summary of Focus Groups and Structured Interviews Listening Systems:

P = Proposed   I = Introduced   E = Established

Guidelines for listening systems: Cyclical, predictable, public (open, transparent), user-friendly

Part III: Web Site

School: Principal: Date: Email:

Web Site Listening	Parents	Teachers and Administrators	Staff	Students	Patrons	P	I	E	Rationale: Current Practice
What do we currently do with the data?									
Authority to act? (commit resources)									
Who?/When?									
How?									

Summary of Web Site Listening Systems:

P = Proposed   I = Introduced   E = Established

Guidelines for listening systems: Cyclical, predictable, public (open, transparent), user-friendly

Plus/Delta (+/Δ) Group Processing Tool

Plus/delta is a very convenient way to reflect on the value of any group process or meeting and to do so in a positive, proactive manner. Here is how it works:

1. Following any group activity, ask someone to serve as a recorder on one side of the room with a flipchart labeled "+."

2. Ask a second person to serve as a recorder on the other side of the room with a flipchart labeled "Δ."

3. Set the ground rules by asking the audience to identify what worked well in the meeting just concluded that warrants repetition in similar future meetings. The responses to that question are recorded on the plus chart.

4. Ask audience members to identify what aspects of the process can be improved. Record suggestions for improvement on the delta chart.

It is important for everyone to understand that this is not a process by which we identify positives or negatives, and that no personal references (even positive) are part of +/Δ. Stick to what events and behaviors are worth replicating, and which events and behaviors could be improved and how.

Note that both plus and delta will yield helpful, instructive feedback and encourage team thinking and proactive planning.

+ Positive Outcomes and Processes	Δ Suggestions to Improve Meetings

Logarithmic Chart
for Forecasting

Think of data in your area of responsibility that you need to predict as accurately as possible. For the data that is time-referenced or must be projected into the future, a logarithmic chart with a best-fit trend line can be two and three times as accurate as an equal-interval chart with the same data.

Data set: _____ Projected timeline: _____ to _____.

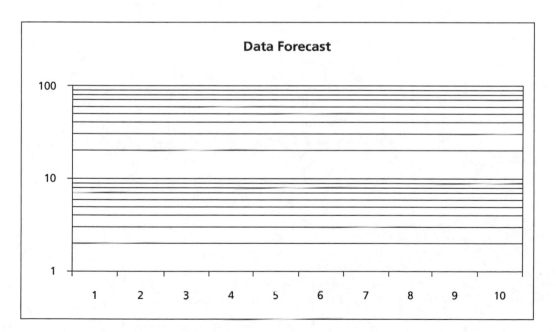

Glossary

Assessment Terms

AYP
adequate yearly progress; term created for Title I schools to monitor improvement gains and extended in the No Child Left Behind Act of 2001 as a measure of improvement gains for all subgroups. Although states develop their own standards, this component serves as a linchpin of accountability in the landmark legislation.

CRT
criterion-referenced test; a test that measures discrete knowledge and skills.

EOC assessments
end-of-course assessments, also known as *common assessments.*

GE
grade equivalent; indicates the year and month of school for which a student's score is typical. A GE of 6.2, for example, indicates that the student is achieving at a level typical of students who have completed the second month of grade 6 at the time the test was standardized. Interpret GEs with caution. A student in grade 3 may attain a GE of 6.2—this does not mean that the student is capable of doing sixth-grade work, only that the student is scoring well above average for grade 3.

IQ
intelligence quotient; a scaled score with 100 representing the population average in terms of the ability to solve verbal, mathematical, and spatial problems.

NAEP
National Assessment of Educational Progress; a comprehensive assessment authorized by Congress to gather samples of student performance on standards in the United States for comparison purposes with students from other nations, track longitudinal trends, and monitor basic skills in core content areas.

NCE
normal curve equivalent; equal-interval scores used to compare achievement across subject areas over time. NCEs provide information that is

more precise regarding raw score performance than the national percentile score, but absent subscale information, offer little to help in diagnosing student performance or designing interventions.

NP   *national percentile;* a scaled score that indicates what percent of participants scored below the individual score reported. A common measure, the NP is often misinterpreted, as the percentile differences are not equal-interval in terms of raw score. NPs compare the achievement of students in a local group with that of students in the nation as a whole.

NRT   *norm-referenced test;* the traditional standardized test that measures students' performance against their peers rather than against standards or criteria.

performance assessment   A demonstration of knowledge, skills, and understanding designed to improve student learning, address standards, and allow students to demonstrate proficiency in multiple ways; generally evaluated by using scoring guides (rubrics).

Parametric Tests

analysis of variance   Method that tests for significant variance resulting from different sources of variation. Its utility lies in the fact that you can determine the relative impact from selected treatments, from error, and from other causes. It is predicated on the assumptions of normality, independence, and parametric data, and yields an F ratio.

multiple regression   Analysis that studies the effects and magnitudes of the effects of more than one independent variable (causes) on one dependent variable. An analysis might examine the relative effects of several instructional strategies on student achievement, yielding an R^2 value for each of the interactions. It is a particularly desirable test of significance because it allows educators to determine the relative impact of several antecedents on a single dependent variable such as student achievement.

Pearson's *r* (product-moment correlation coefficient)   A very reliable estimate of correlation that tests the relationship between two parametric variables, yielding a coefficient between -1.0 for a perfect negative correlation to $+1.0$ for a perfect positive correlation. This powerful tool allows us to plot the relationship between any two variables using a simple graph with X and Y axes, and is particularly useful in determining the relationship between cause and effect.

relationships between cause and effect   Correlation is not causation, particularly given the complex process of teaching and learning. Strong correlations are related to the effect, and given sufficient and repeated research findings, the initial correlation may be eventually recognized as a cause. For example, fifty years ago smoking was recognized as having only a correlation to lung cancer; over time (and the objections of tobacco lobbyists), smoking was eventually recognized as the primary cause of lung cancer. In the same way, correlations allow us to examine relationships to teaching and learning and make decisions that improve student achievement without waiting to determine absolute causation.

Relationships between causes (conditions, teaching strategies, resources, time, programs, protocols, and adult actions), and effects (student achievement results) reveal three types of relationships: positive, negative, and none. By plotting causes on an X (horizontal) axis and effects on a Y (vertical) axis, we can visibly depict relationships and compute a Pearson's r. Positive correlations show an increase in the effect variable when there is an increase in the cause variable; this displays graphically as a chart with a trend line from the lower left quadrant to the upper right. The opposite is true for a negative correlation, where an increase in the cause variable produces a decline in the effect variable, or movement from the upper left quadrant to the lower right. The third type of relationship is no relationship at all, depicted graphically by a scattering of responses and a trend line that moves from left to right without direction up or down in terms of the effect (Y, vertical) variable. Calculation of an R^2 allows educators to determine both positive and negative relationships in terms of their relative strength rather than positive or negative direction. All three types provide meaningful information to assist in informed and effective decisionmaking.

t test Used to determine whether two means are significantly different for different sample size. Data is assumed to be interval or ratio data; the test is particularly useful in comparing means for samples smaller than thirty subjects per variable.

Nonparametric Tests

chi-square (x^2) A nonparametric test that compares proportions observed with proportions expected to see if they are significantly different. It is a very useful statistic to measure classroom, department, or school performance, especially when comparing proportions of students not meeting standards, progressing, proficient, and advanced on state assessments.

Friedman F_r test A rank-order analysis-of-variance test that can be used to identify preferences among several options.

Kruskal-Wallis test A nonparametric test of significance that uses sums of ranks within variables to determine relative differences on a single criterion using irregular data; yields the Kruskal-Wallis H statistic.

sign test A simple test of significance that compares paired observations on the basis of deviation from the median to determine differences between samples.

Sources: Kerlinger, 1986, 449–467; Downing & Clark, 1997, x, 297.

References

Ainsworth, L. (2003). *Unwrapping the standards.* Englewood, CO: Advanced Learning Press.

Andersen, B., & Fagerhaug, T. (2000). *Root cause analysis: Simplified tools and techniques.* Milwaukee: ASQ Quality Press.

Auman, L., & Young, K. (2004, September). What's happening at school? (unpublished manuscript); telephone conversation with author.

Bernhardt, V. (2000, Winter). New routes open when one type of data crosses another. *Journal of Staff Development, 21,* 34.

Britannica Concise Encyclopedia. (2004). s.v. "proof."

Calhoun, E. F. (1994). *How to use action research in the self-renewing school.* Alexandria, VA: ASCD.

Center for Performance Assessment [CPA]. (2004). "Data Teams" seminar. Denver, CO.

Covey, Stephen. (1996). *The seven habits of highly effective people.* New York: Simon & Schuster.

Danielson, C. (1996). *Enhancing professional practice: A framework for teaching.* Alexandria, VA: ASCD.

Darling-Hammond, L. (1997). *The right to learn.* San Francisco: Jossey-Bass.

Deming, W. Edwards. (2000). *The new economics for industry, government, education* (2d ed.). Cambridge, MA: MIT Press.

Downing, D., & Clark, J. (1997). *Statistics the easy way* (3d ed.). New York: Barron's.

Evans, R. (1996). *The human side of school change: Reform, resistance, and the real-life problems of innovation.* San Francisco: Jossey-Bass.

Fredricks, J. A., Blumenfeld, P. B., & Parks, A. (2004, Spring). School engagement: Potential of the concept, state of the evidence. *Review of Educational Research, 74*(1), 59–109.

Fulghum, R. (1989). *All I really need to know I learned in kindergarten.* New York: Villard Books.

Fullan, M. (2001). *Leading in a culture of change.* San Francisco: Jossey-Bass.

Graham, S., Harris, K. R., Fink-Chorzempa, B., & MacArthur, C. (2003, June). Primary grade teachers' instructional adaptations for struggling writers: A national survey. *Journal of Educational Psychology, 95,* 279–292.

Gregory, G. H., & Chapman, C. (2002). *Differentiated instructional strategies: One size doesn't fit all.* Thousand Oaks, CA: Corwin Press.

Heacox, D. (2002). *Differentiating instruction in the regular classroom: How to reach and teach all learners, grades 3–12.* Minneapolis, MN: Free Spirit Publishing.

Holcomb, E. (2004). *Getting excited about data: Combining people, passion, and proof to maximize student achievement* (2d ed.). Thousand Oaks, CA: Corwin Press.

Kerlinger, F. N. (1986). *Foundations of behavioral research* (3d ed.). New York: Holt, Rinehart, & Winston.

Marzano, R. J., Pickering, D. J., & Pollock, J. E. (2001a). *Classroom instruction that works: Research-based strategies for increasing student achievement.* Alexandria, VA: ASCD.

Marzano, R. J., Pickering, D. J., & Pollock, J. E. (2001b). *A handbook for classroom instruction that works.* ASCD: Alexandria, VA.

Merriam-Webster's collegiate dictionary (11th ed.). (2003). s.v. "analysis," p. 44.

Mickey, K., ed. (2003, March 31). Publishers scurry to amass proof that instructional materials work—Educational publishers are looking for research that validates their products. *Educational Marketer, 34*(10), 3–4.

Public Law No. 107-110. (2002). No Child Left Behind Act of 2001.

Raymond, M. E. (2003, December 3). Track the relationship between teachers and their students. *Charlotte Observer (N.C.)/Hoover Institution.*

Reeves, D. B. (2004a) *Accountability for learning: How teachers and school leaders take charge.* Alexandria, VA: ASCD.

Reeves, D. B. (2004b). *Accountability in action* (2d ed.). Englewood, CO: Advanced Learning Press, ch. 19.

Reeves, D. B. (2004c). *Assessing educational leaders.* Thousand Oaks, CA: Corwin Press.

Reeves, D. B. (2002). *Reason to write: Help your child succeed in school and in life through better reasoning and clear communication.* New York: Simon & Schuster.

Sanders, W. L. (1998, December). Value-added assessment: A method for measuring the effects of the system, school and teacher on the rate of student academic progress. *The School Administrator* (Web edition); retrieved July 17, 2004 from http://www.aasa.org/publications/sa/1998_12/sanders.htm.

Schlechty, P. C. (2001). *Shaking up the school house: How to support and sustain educational innovation.* San Francisco: Jossey-Bass.

Schmoker, M. (1999). *Results: The key to continuous improvement in education* (2d ed.). Alexandria, VA: ASCD.

Senge, P. (2000). *Schools that learn.* New York: Doubleday.

Sparks, D. (2004, March). Closing the knowing-doing gap requires acting on what we already know. *Results, 7*(6), 1–2.

Steiner, L. (2000). A review of the research literature on scaling up in education: The problem of scaling-up in education. Chicago, IL: North Central Regional Educational Laboratory. Available at http://www.ncrel.org/csri/resources/scaling/review.htm

Sternberg, R. J. (2004). What is an expert student? *Educational Researcher, 32*(8), 5–9.

Sunderman, G. L., Tracey, C. A., Kim, J., & Orfield, G. (2004). *Listening to teachers: Classroom realities and No Child Left Behind.* Cambridge, MA: The Civil Rights Project at Harvard University.

Surowiecki, J. (2004). *The wisdom of crowds: Why the many are smarter than the few and how collective wisdom shapes business, economies, societies, and nations.* New York: Doubleday.

Tomlinson, C. A. (2001). *How to differentiate instruction in mixed-ability classrooms* (2d ed.). Alexandria, VA: ASCD.

Wenglinsky, H. (2002, February 13). How schools matter: The link between teacher classroom practices and student academic performance. *Education Policy Analysis Archives, 10*(12), 6–31.

White, S. (2005). *Beyond the numbers.* Englewood, CO: Advanced Learning Press.

Index

A

accountability, 11–16, 34, 81
  acts of, 13–15, 103
  barriers to, 13–15
  data analysis methods and, 64
  embedding, 37
  lack of, 35
  scoring guide matrix, 110–112
  structures, 51–52, 86
  triangulation and, 67, 76
action, 8, 94
  after analysis, 25
  authority to take, 12, 76, 81–82
  comparisons, 17
  of discovery, 52
  responsibility to take, 11, 12, 76
  verbs of, 29
action research, 49, 51, 60–62, 65
  after data analysis, 77
  replication and, 80–81
adequate yearly progress (AYP), 59, 60
Ainsworth, Larry, 27
analysis methods
  scoring guide matrix, 112–114
antecedents (of excellence), 2, 10–11, 34
  accountability and, 11
  data analysis methods and, 51–52, 64
  identifying, 30, 86
  proven, 3, 26–27
  relationships to strategies and achievement, 61

replicating. *See* replication
  scoring guide matrix, 108–109
  triangulation and, 67
  understanding, 11, 30
assessment calendars, 8–10, 102
assumptions, unlearning, 2
Auman, Linda, 2
authority
  accountability and, 13, 16
  for action, 12, 76, 81–82
  for subtraction, 44, 76, 81–82
autonomy, 1, 58

B

Bernhardt, Victoria, 33–34
best practices, 2, 3, 83
burden of proof, 3–4

C

Calhoun, Emily, 80
"canaries." *See* monitoring
candor, 5, 37, 57
cause-and-effect analysis, 153
causes, 10
Center for Performance Assessment, 2, 61
  "Data Team" seminar, 17
  "Making Standards Work" model, 58
central tendency measures, 62
chance, 23, 24
change
  cultural, 38

change *(continued)*
  culture for, 44
  delaying, 79
  drivers of, 52
  threat from, 60
checklist for integrated decision making, 6, 8
chi-square test, 69
clarification analysis, 49, 51, 60, 61, 145
Clark, J., 93
class size, 6, 10
collaboration, 5–10, 26, 34
  accountability and, 11
  checklist, 97
  data analysis methods and, 64
  meetings for, 92
  scoring guide matrix, 109–110
  structures, 51–52
  tools for, 5
  triangulation and, 67, 76
  weakness in, 35
collective wisdom, 6
communication, 52
  with parents, 38
  of values, 86
continuous improvement, 49, 51, 62–65
  in meetings, 92
  replication and, 83
control charts, 60, 62–63, 157–158
Cornell notes, 60
Covey, Stephen, 79
criterion-referenced tests (CRTs), 8, 9
critical incident analysis, 5–6, 8, 95–96
  as initial tool, 57
curriculum alignment, 6, 7, 86
curriculum modification, 38

D
data
  accountability and, 13
  application to teaching, 21
  availability of, 29, 69
  defining by purpose, 24–25
  embedded, 125
  existing, 51–52
  incomplete, 69
  linkage to action, 25
  soft, 96
  time-referenced, 93

types of, 6, 19, 21, 22–23, 24–25, 28
data analysis, 8, 12, 30–31
  insights from, 21
  methods, 49–65, 112–114
  multiple data points, 34
  norms for, 57, 58, 155–156
  pattern identification, 62, 69
  perfection in, 69
  principles of, 4–16
  purposes of, 77
  replication and, 83
  scoring guide matrix for, 107–119
  skills in, 4
  template, 134
  tools, 5, 63, 86, 94
  validity of, 28
data capture, 33
data collection, 8, 11, 21
  means for, 17, 41–42
  purposes of, 31
  quantity of data, 33
  sources of data, 37, 41–42
  systematic, 26
data intersections, 33–35
data management, 77, 108
  improving system, 42
  scoring guide matrix, 108
  strategies, 46
data of improving, 25, 26, 30, 42, 43
data of learning, 26, 27–28, 42, 43
data of persuading, 25, 26, 30, 42, 43, 44
data of teaching, 25–27, 42
data road map, 33–47
  template, 121–132
data teams, 17–18, 37, 105–106
data walls, 80, 83
data-driven decision making (DDDM), 33
  changes to system for, 126
  principles of, 4–16
decision making, 8
  data-driven. *See* data-driven decision making
  integrated, 6, 8
  prioritizing, 58
decisionmaking analysis, 49, 50, 58–60
decision matrix, 143
Deming, W. Edwards, 85
demographics, student, 54

dichotomous data, 22, 24
differences, analysis of, 62
discrepancy charts, 77–79, 157–158
Downing, D., 93
drivers, 6, 99

E
effectiveness, measures of, 1, 25
    external, 18
    teacher-developed, 2
environmental scan, 52, 54, 55–56
evidence. *See also* data
    acceptance of, 2–3
    of benefit, 83
    preponderance of, 1
    of success, 79

F
faculty. *See* teachers
feedback, 17, 26
    corrective, 38, 85
    data road map, 40, 124
    gathering, 86
    plus/delta tool for, 92
field trips, 53
Fink-Chorzempa, B., 2
Flagg, Flora, 61
flowcharts and flowcharting, 52, 53, 135–138
force-field analysis, 54, 57–58, 59, 141–142
forecasting, 93
Fulghum, Robert, 27

G
goals, 86
    barriers to achievement of, 58–59, 86
Graham, S., 2
graphic organizers, 27–28

H
Harris, K. R., 2
Hishakawa Fishbone, 54, 57, 62, 65, 153
Holcomb, Edie, 4, 34
hunches, 61
hypotheses, 23, 24, 60

I
implementation
    lack of, 2

level of, 86
    scheduling, 8–10
    of standards, 10
    timelines, 45
improvement, 86
    continuous. *See* continuous improvement
    data of. *See* data of improving
    data road map for, 45
    explicitness for, 46
    meetings, 92
    in work habits/routines, 35–36, 38,
        63–65, 92
indicators, 6, 99
innovation, 77, 79, 82
    promoting, 86, 92
instructional program, structuring, 4
instructional strategies and practices, 61
    as antecedents, 10
    effectiveness of, 35
    modifying, 37, 38
    replicable, 77, 79. *See also* replication
    student input re, 44
    verification of, 16
interval data, 22–23, 24

J
judgment, professional, 8, 67

K
knowing-doing gap, 2
KWL (Know, Want, Learn) strategy, 38, 54,
    148

L
leadership, 76
    acts of, 85–86, 94
    assessment of, 85
    building, 44
    curriculum alignment with standards, 86
    data road map, 130
    effectiveness of, 11
    scoring guide matrix, 117–119
    by teachers, 11
Leadership and Learning Matrix, 10, 11
learning
    conditions for, 2
    data of. *See* data of learning
    measures of, 27

learning *(continued)*
    third-person, 79
learning gap, 1, 16
learning objectives, 2
listening systems, 86, 88–92, 162–164
logarithmic chart, 93, 167

M
MacArthur, C., 2
meetings
    norms for, 57, 58, 155–156
    plus/delta tool for improving, 92
    "What's working?", 80, 83
mini-lessons, 2, 17
monitoring, 17–18
    actions, 28
    control charts for, 63
    data road map, 125
    early warning indicators, 38
    existing improvement plans, 33
    methods of, 28
multivariate analyses, 69

N
90/90/90 schools, 61
No Child Left Behind (NCLB) Act of 2001,
    1, 18
    effects of, 6
    research requirements, 4
nominal data, 22, 24
nonparametric data and tests, 22, 24, 171
nostalgia, 16, 37
note-taking strategies, 60
null hypothesis, 23, 24

O
ordinal data, 22, 24
overtesting, 10

P
parametric data, 22, 23–24
parametric tests, 24, 170–171
performance. *See* student achievement
performance measures, 26
    institutionalizing use of, 40
    rubric-based, 74
    teacher-developed, 28
persuasion, data of. *See* data of persuading

plus/delta group processing tool, 92–93,
    165–166
practices. *See* best practices; instructional
    strategies and practices
process map. *See* flowcharts and flowcharting
professional development, 6, 7
proficiency, opportunities to achieve, 28
progress reports, 38–39
projections, 93
proof, 2, 3–4, 19. *See also* evidence

Q
quality, 85

R
ratio data, 23, 24
rearview-mirror effect, 4, 16, 17
    data road map, 122
    minimizing/avoiding, 17, 28, 33, 37–38
recommendations, 8
Reeves, Douglas, 2, 4, 11
reflection, 8
relations diagram, 6–8, 99–100
relationships, 62
    discovering, 6, 61
    measure of, 62
replication, 54, 77–83
    action research for, 60
    of meeting behaviors/practices, 92
    of proven practices, 2
    scoring guide matrix, 116
    strategies for, 79, 80
report cards for schools, 6
resource allocation and commitment, 44,
    81–82
root-cause analysis, 6
routines, 35–36. *See also* work habits
run charts, 157–158

S
scales of measurement, 69
scattergram, 62
Schmoker, Mike, 4
scoring guide matrix, 19, 107–119
Senge, Peter, 52
side-by-side analysis, 86, 87, 160
significance, statistical, 23, 24
solutions method of analysis, 49, 50, 54

force-field analysis in, 57–58
stakeholders, 86, 92
standards
    deviation from, 157–158
    focus on, 40
    implementing, 10
    of proof, 3–4, 19
    "unwrapping" of, 27
state assessments (annual)
    reliance on, 16, 37
    uses of, 1–2
    waiting for, 79
statistical analysis, 62
statistical significance, 23, 24
statistics, 21
Steiner, Lucy, 2
student achievement, 1, 34
    antecedents of. See antecedents
    focus on, 16, 63, 85–86
    measures of, 11, 16, 29
    relationships to strategies and antecedents,
        61
    risks to, 59
    teaching and, 25–27
    understanding of, 26
student behaviors, 10
subgroups, 1, 86
subtraction, 11, 13, 16
    authority for, 44, 76, 81–82
    data road map, 124
    what to delete, 40–41, 77, 82
Surowiecki, James, 2
SWOT (strengths, weaknesses, opportunities,
        threats) analysis, 17–18, 105–106
system, 52
systems analysis, 49, 50, 52–54
    systems within systems, 52

T
teachers
    behaviors, 2, 10. See also instructional
        strategies and practices; work habits
    effectiveness measures, 12
    expectations of, 86
    influence of, 30
    view of scrutiny and standards, 1
team thinking, 5, 44, 57, 92
technology literacy, 10

test scores, 1, 18. See also student
        achievement
testing, 10
textbook selection, 6, 7
thinking
    higher-order, 2, 27
    team, 5, 44, 57, 92
Tier 1 data, 19
Tier 2 data, 19
Tier 3 data, 19, 79
time allocation, 8, 12–13, 39
trends, 69, 94
triangulation, 34, 35, 67–76, 95
    data included in, 86
    exercise, 70–72
    scoring guide matrix, 115
    template, 147–148
    for verification, 67–69
2 × 2 matrix, 62

V
values, 58, 86, 92
variables, 23, 62, 93
    multiple, 69, 74
variance, 157–158
    analysis of, 62
Venn diagrams, 63–65, 139–140
verification, 8, 81

W
wagon wheel, 69, 73–75, 76
    template, 150–151
warning signs. See monitoring
wisdom, collective, 6
Woodson, Nan, 60
work habits, 35–36
    evidence capture by, 79
    improving, 35–36, 38, 63–65, 92
worksheets, 2
writing, 2, 26

Y
Young, Karen, 2

Z
zero point, 23, 77, 93
zero tolerance, 63

Do you believe all students can succeed?

Can educators make a difference and produce results?

So much to do and so little time!

Since 1992, school districts and educational organizations seeking to improve student achievement have consulted with Douglas Reeves and his colleagues at the Center for Performance Assessment. Educational leaders on five continents have collaboratively created customized solutions based on research and results. If you would like to know more about the services of the Center for Performance Assessment, to learn about success stories for every type of educational setting, to find out about the latest research, or to arrange a presentation by Douglas Reeves, please visit the Web site at *www.MakingStandardsWork.com* or contact:

CENTER FOR PERFORMANCE ASSESSMENT

Success for every student.

317 Inverness Way South, Suite 150 ▪ Englewood, CO 80112
(800) 844-6599 or (303) 504-9312 ▪ Fax (303) 504-9417